C000268792

SHAMANISM

Inspiring | Educating | Creating | Entertaining

Brimming with creative inspiration, how-to projects, and useful information to enrich your everyday life, Quarto Knows is a favorite destination for those pursuing their interests and passions. Visit our site and dig deeper with our books into your area of interest: Quarto Creates, Quarto Cooks, Quarto Homes, Quarto Lives, Quarto Drives, Quarto Explores, Quarto Gifts, or Quarto Kids.

Copyright © 2020 by Zambezi Publishing Ltd.
Text © 2020 by Zambezi Publishing Ltd.
Unless otherwise noted on page 144 illustrations © 2018 Quarto Publishing Group USA Inc.

First published in 2020 by Wellfleet Press,
an imprint of The Quarto Group
142 West 36th Street, 4th Floor
New York, NY 10018, USA
T (212) 779-4972 F (212) 779-6058
www.QuartoKnows.com

10 9 8 7 6 5 4 3

ISBN: 978-1-57715-223-1

Library of Congress Control Number: 2020945682

Publisher: Rage Kindelsperger
Creative Director: Laura Drew
Managing Editor: Cara Donaldson
Senior Editor: John Foster
Cover and Interior Design: Ashley Prine, Tandem Books

Printed in China

This book provides general information on various widely known and widely accepted images that tend to evoke feelings of strength and confidence. However, it should not be relied upon as recommending or promoting any specific diagnosis or method of treatment for a particular condition, and it is not intended as a substitute for medical advice or for direct diagnosis and treatment of a medical condition by a qualified physician. Readers who have questions about a particular condition, possible treatments for that condition, or possible reactions from the condition or its treatment should consult a physician or other qualified healthcare professional.

IN FOCUS

SHAMANISM

Your Personal Guide

TRACIE LONG

WELLFLEET
PRESS

CONTENTS

AN INTRODUCTION TO

SHAMANISM

The word *shaman* in general terms means "one who sees" or "one who knows," and it's thought to have originated from the Tungus people of Siberia, who call such people *šamān*. Shamans are highly respected people within their communities or tribes because they provide wisdom, healing, rite-of-passage ceremonies, counseling, and knowledge. They tend to either come from a lineage of shamans or be chosen by spirit; it can take many years of teaching to become a shaman and to learn how to work with the land and with elements and nature. Shamans believe that everything has a spirit and that everything is connected. They also use altered states of consciousness to call upon spirit guides, ancestors, animal totems, and guardians while they seek to bring back harmony and balance to the land, the tribe, or an individual person.

Shamans see illness as loss of power, which they work to return to their patients—especially when it has been lost during their lives through loss or trauma, although in some cases, the loss of power can link back to past-life issues. The shaman will remove unwanted energy or unneeded blockages from the body, a process called shamanic extraction. The energy may not be inherently bad but rather misplaced, and because it is not meant to be in the body, it shows up as pain, illness, or emotional problems.

A Tungus shaman

Shamans work with the spirit or the soul of a person so their healing takes place at "soul level." They obtain their knowledge by working with their spiritual guides, which include animal guides, through shifting their state of awareness, and in some cases they connect to those whom they are healing through journeying, drumming, and medicines, or by seeing the patient through the eyes of their guides.

Sometimes the shaman may perform a soul retrieval. Soul loss can happen after a traumatic experience, such as an accident, during which part of the soul leaves the body in order to protect itself. Unfortunately, the lost part of the soul doesn't always return, so the person may live on for a long time feeling that part of them is missing.

Shamans can look into past lives. They put their patient into a meditative state and then take them back to a time when the patient experienced something that may now be contributing to a mental or physical health problem. When the patient journeys along with the shaman, they are able to pinpoint the issue and to make sense of it. Often, knowing the cause helps the patient to take back their power and start healing themselves because they now understand where the issue stems from.

What Is Shamanism?

Shamanism is a form of spirituality that seeks to expand one's consciousness. While many people associate it with North and South America, it has been practiced all over the world, including in Asia, Africa, Europe, and Australasia. Shamanism still flourishes today in the Andes and the Amazon, and traditional healers abound in southern Africa. They have different names in different cultures, but whatever they are called, their methods are strikingly similar all over the world.

Shamans are commonly known to be healers and spiritual guiders. Through history, they were healers at first, then teachers, visionaries, and mystics. Each shaman is different and each works in their own unique way. There are shamans who care for the earth and nature and weather shamans who work to bring rain or warmth when it is needed. There are those who help to heal the sick and others who assist the dead on their journey back to the spirit world.

Shamans serve as intermediaries between this world and others and for the connections between all living things. It takes them many years to develop their spiritual sight and learn to find answers in the invisible world that connects us. When trained, they can draw upon the relationships that they have formed with their guides and traverse realms, acquiring the knowledge, information, and assistance needed for rituals and ceremonies. They can decipher symbols and understand what they represent or use them as tools of empowerment. A symbol may be interpreted many ways, but each shaman has their own method of interpretation.

Shamans can put themselves into a trancelike state that enables them to move between states of consciousness at will, and they do this by singing, dancing, meditating, and drumming. Animals often play an important role, acting as omens and message bearers as well as representations of the animal spirit guides. While the shaman is performing a ceremony, their spirit leaves their body and enters the spiritual realms, enabling them to perform certain tasks.

Interest in shamanism has grown in recent years, and the subject attracts many spiritual seekers. There are shamanic schools and foundations that teach courses and hold workshops, and it has even become part of the tourist industry, with teachers and practitioners taking groups to destinations in the Andes and the Amazon to work with established shamans. Some shamans are happy to open their doors to teach those outside their culture how to expand knowledge of their spiritual path, in addition to holding ceremonies and performing rituals. Their courses often include learning about healing and medicine techniques.

But you don't have to book a trip or go on a spiritual quest to learn the basic techniques; they are easy to learn, and you just need a little self-discipline and dedication. You may start by teaching yourself from a book, but if you want to develop your skills, you will need to find a real shaman who can give you instruction.

Altered States of Consciousness

Altered states of perception can be measured with electroencephalography (EEG), which shows us the number of brain-wave cycles, or rhythmic pulses of neural activity, the brain produces every second. The normal oscillation of a beta wave in an adult is between thirteen and thirty-eight cycles per second, and the alpha wave oscillation is about eight to twelve cycles per second when a person is relaxed or meditating. This is "being in the here and now." Theta waves oscillate at four to seven cycles per second, and they become dominant just before we fall asleep, during lucid dreaming, or when we reach a deep trance state during meditation or journeying. Delta waves oscillate at less than four cycles per second when we are asleep.

We can all learn to alter our state of consciousness by practicing meditation, but some may want to take it further so they can have out-of-body experiences or try lucid dreaming. Lucid dreaming is when one chooses something to dream about, falls into a kind of daydream or trance state, then falls asleep and continues with the chosen dream on occasion.

Other Roles in Shamanism

A shaman may be called upon to heal someone who feels lost or depressed and can help to restore the patient back to health because shamanic practice works for mental health as well as physical health. The shaman may "journey," or conduct a ceremony for this, because they will need to be in an altered state in order to form a diagnosis and to restore the person's power and bring the patient back to a state of harmony.

Journeying

Journeying is a form of meditation that is used to take the practitioner or teacher, their students, and even their patients away from the normal state of consciousness that exists in all our daily lives and allow them to "travel" into an altered state.

You can try journeying yourself at home, as it is a form of meditation done to drumming. This can be done alone or with others such as in a group class. In formal groups, the rhythmic drumming may last up to an hour. Drumming promotes relaxation and helps to allow the journeyers to relax and allow images or thoughts to enter their minds. As with so many spiritual practices, it is always worth setting one's intention.

Perhaps you want to try journeying because there is something you need to find out or answers you want to be given. The answers may be shown to you in different ways each time you take a spiritual journey, so it would be a good idea to keep a journal of all the information you gather. Not all of it will make sense at first, but after a time it will.

Learn more about journeying on page 21.

Tip

Setting an intention means knowing and saying what you want to achieve before setting out on the journey or performing a ceremony or ritual.

How to Use This Book

The shamanism described in this book is a mixture of modern and traditional practices that, unless noted, are not associated with any particular tribe or culture. On these pages, I tell you what shamanism is all about, how to use it, and, in particular, how to carry out shamanic healing in a safe way.

A Note about Safety and Controversial Shamanic Practices

It is well known that shamans the world over use methods that are not safe and that I don't wish to talk about or recommend to anyone. However, it is worth bearing in mind that a great many unpleasant or unsafe practices have existed in the past, and some can still be found in traditional practices in certain countries.

Enclosed Shamanism Wall Chart

Included in this book is a wall chart that serves as a quick and handy reference guide to the essential information about shamanism found on the following pages.

1

HISTORICAL BACKGROUND

Human beings came into existence in the Rift Valley in Africa, and over time they spread out to different parts of Africa and the Middle East. Climatic change meant that the migrating humans died out, but about a thousand humans continued to survive in the warm and fertile Rift Valley. Further migrations took place, and eventually humans managed to establish themselves permanently in various parts of the world.

The San are one of the oldest groups of humans. They lived in various parts of southern Africa since the dawn of humankind, and they may indeed be an offshoot of the early migrators from the Rift Valley.

The development of specialized roles within a society can only really occur when people take up agriculture, corral animals for their use, and settle into villages. It is then that some members of the group can be spared from the continual work of hunting and gathering to perform jobs that are suited to their temperaments and specialized talents. However, even among ancient nomadic peoples, some special skills were still prized, and we know from carvings and cave paintings that some were artistic. We also know there were shamans at work way back in time, because some San cave paintings that are

A San cave painting

> ## Tip
>
> The pronunciation of *muti* rhymes with "sooty." Southern Africans from many cultures call all types of traditional medicines, ointments, and lotions muti to this day.

more than seventy thousand years old depict humans wearing animal heads or animal masks and clearly working as shamans!

Shamanic practices have been recorded among every nomadic group in the world, and cave paintings in France and Spain show them at work in that region as far back as forty thousand years. We know that the stargazing that led to astrology is over thirty thousand years old, and that also seems to be part of some shamanic traditions. For the most part, shamanism seems to have been natural for ancient nomadic peoples, because they could work on the move and could intercede between daily life on earth and the world of spirits.

The word *shaman* derives from the word *šamān*, which is a Tungusic word that seems to translate as "one who knows." Although variations of this word appear in many languages, many others have their own terms for those who follow shamanistic practices. Sangomas, for example, are respected healers of the Zulu people in South Africa who practice traditional shamanic healing in addition to prescribing medicine, called *muti*, for their patients.

Modern History

As centuries passed and more and more people became nonnomadic, specialized priests began to work in special buildings to do this healing work on behalf of the communities who that served. They trained in particular beliefs and methods and weren't supposed to deviate too much from them, while shamans continued to do what seemed to work best under their local circumstances. The remarkable thing is that shamanic practices the world over were and are very similar.

Typically, a shaman connects to the "other world" in order to heal the sick, to remedy any problems that the tribe is experiencing, and to help the dying to cross over in peace. It involves tapping into help from gods, spirits, and maybe even demons. People don't choose to become shamans but are "called" to their vocation by a spiritual experience, possibly a traumatic one in childhood. Often this is a near-death experience that takes them to the afterlife and back again, or it may be a tragic loss that opens the door to the spiritual world.

Many shamanic practices place emphasis on drumming, dancing, and other forms of rhythmic music to help create an altered state of consciousness in the shaman and sometimes also in those who consult them. Though these practices are similar the world over, the history of shamanism and the particulars of its practices in each place are different. Here are just some examples.

The Americas

In North America, shamans were traditionally prophets who predicted the outcome of the hunt, helped find lost objects, and worked out the root cause of any ill will in the community. They were consulted at times of sickness and bad fortune. Shamans from the Blackfoot, Cree, and Ojibwa tribes were known to make prophecies while in trance states during certain ceremonies.

Amazingly, South American shamans as far south as Tierra del Fuego share some practices with the Inuit and Siberian peoples of the far north. This shows shamanism has maintained beliefs and practices over centuries and despite traveling great distances. South American shamans connect with spirit helpers, sometimes using crystals for healing. They also believe in soul retrieval, which you will see more of later in this book. They use rattles and drums, and like Native American shamans from North America, they try to create harmony and balance within their local population.

In the Caribbean, Haitian Vodou started life in West Africa and migrated to the West Indies with slavery. It is a combination of a religion, ancestor worship, spellcasting, clearing bad spells, and healing the sick. It involves drumming and singing and groups who work on problems while in a trance. Another version of Caribbean spirituality is Jamaican Obeah, which involves using supernatural powers.

Europe

Spiritual people who tap into the universe for healing purposes or who give people help and guidance with the aid of spirits have always existed in Europe. Various pagan religions and beliefs have come and gone, and some have reappeared in one form or another. Shamanic healers now exist in Europe, and there are people who perform soul retrieval here. (I should know because I am one of them!)

Asia

The Itako shamans of Japan are elderly women who are blind or very visually impaired. Like mediums the world over, these women can pass messages from those who have passed to bereaved relatives, and they can contact ancient gods to help them heal the physically sick and the sick at heart. There is a four-day festival in late July where Itako women sit in blue tents and give readings to those who come to consult them.

Shamanism is Korea's oldest belief system and it is still alive and well today. Korean shamans are women who have been called to the vocation, often after living through some trauma. They light candles, use incense, ring bells, use drums, and sometimes walk on sharp objects when in a trance. The purpose is to heal people by removing bad spirits that have entered a sick or unhappy person. Some of their practices are violent and can seem strange to Westerners, but they are familiar to spiritual people the world over.

So wherever we look in the world, whether among ancient societies or the most modern, we can find shamanism alive and well and making itself useful. While this book takes a modern view of shamanism, it also explores traditional practices that are still used today.

2

THE SHAMANIC WORLDS

The shamanic world is divided into three levels—the lower world, the middle world, and the upper world—which are all connected via the cosmic tree, also known as the tree of life. The levels are timeless and infinite, so prolonged hypnotic drumming is often used to promote relaxation that will help to move between them. Once the practitioner is in an alternative state of awareness, it opens them up to finding more insight, wisdom, and knowledge.

The lower world can be used for healing, self-empowerment, meeting animal guides, and delving into past-life issues. This is where we find the "shadows"— our shadow selves, and our spirit souls, which live there. This area usually shows itself in journeying as forests, rivers, deserts, and mountains.

The middle world is where spiritual beings live, and these guides and helpers are always ready to work with those who are able to connect with them. This will help students of shamanism to enhance their abilities and to expand their spiritual knowledge. This realm is used mostly to communicate with plants, the sun, the moon, and other elements of nature. This is where healing takes place, synchronicities are observed, and telepathy and mediumship are possible.

The upper world is the place to go for wisdom and teaching. It's here we find ancestral sprits, ascended masters, and angelic beings. Shamanic teachers recommend that we go here to connect with our higher selves.

When one is studying shamanism or learning how to do shamanic journeys, a teacher will, over time, take the student to all three levels. The teacher will use various meditations or journeys that will enable students to meet their spiritual guides, which include power animals, higher beings, and spirit helpers.

Spirit Guides

Spiritual guides can be people who have lived in the past and now give us help and guidance from the other side. Shamanism also often uses spirit animals for this purpose, and the terms power animals, animal guides, spirit animals, and totem animals are interchangeable, because they all mean some kind of guide who helps us when we need it.

The general belief is that we each have one totem animal that accompanies us throughout life, but other totem animals come and go as needed, and these animals have special abilities that we can tap into when we need their help. This is exactly what the shaman does for us, as they help us to meet our totem animals and to understand their usefulness to us. For instance, if you feel the presence of a squirrel near you, be sure to save some money, because, just as the squirrel hides seeds and nuts in the summer to see him through the winter, you will soon need something to fall back on.

The Levels of Perception

Shamans also believe that we have four levels of perception: the physical level, the emotional and mental level, the soul level, and the spirit level. Each is represented by the energy of a different animal. We all need to become aware of the level at which we are functioning and work on all the levels to reach our highest possible level of spiritual knowledge.

- The physical level is represented by the Serpent, with its natural instinct for sensing approaching danger and its ability to shed its skin, therefore a transformation in itself.

- The emotional and mental level is represented by the Jaguar, the hunter that stalks its prey with thoughtful planning and is quick to adapt. This animal can help us to change and adjust our way of thinking.

- The soul level is represented by the Hummingbird. This tiny bird helps us to achieve our soul journey and the journeys we take in order to see visions or for rituals and ceremonial work. This animal helps us obtain spiritual knowledge and enlightenment.

- The spirit level is represented by the Eagle, which soars high above in order to see the bigger picture. This is also called the level of spiritual enlightenment, where we become able to see all things.

When setting your intentions and planning your meditations or journeying, it might be useful to call upon one of these as your power animal or your animal guide to help you find answers or gain hidden knowledge.

Exercise:
How to Take a Shamanic Journey

What other traditions call meditating or contemplating is known as journeying in the shamanic tradition. If you take these journeys yourself, in time you can expect to feel more creative, passionate, self-aware, wise, and healthy. They are usually done lying down, in semidarkness with your eyes closed in a quiet, safe, and warm environment.

I suggest you have a pillow and a blanket, because your body temperature can drop as you relax, and after a time you may start to feel a little cold. Burn some sage before you start in order to prepare yourself, or maybe do a little ritual. Keep some water nearby as well as a notepad and pen.

I suggest you keep a journal for your journeys, because what you experience won't always make sense right away. It can take time to digest the information given or shown to you, and if you don't write it down, you probably won't remember it all. Plus it's interesting to look back at the animal guides and other helpers you've met and to review the messages you've received, because you're very unlikely to get the same information or even take the same journey every time.

Your first journeys will be to meet your guides. Start by lying somewhere quiet where you know that you won't be disturbed, such as on your bed or couch. Close the curtains. Before you begin, always ask for protection from your guides by asking them to surround you in a dome of white light; do this every time so it becomes a habit.

Now just close your eyes and ask your guides to come forward so that you can sense them. You might get a tingling feeling on your left or right side or around the top of your head. You can instruct them how to present themselves, so they know what you are comfortable with. After some time, you will get to know the sensation of how they make themselves known to you.

Tip

As you begin your shamanic journeys, you will have to develop your senses and learn to recognize the energies of your spirit guides when they are around you and trust whatever you may experience, sense, or feel. This can be images, feelings, or intuitive words. When you close your eyes, you may see patterns or shapes. Everyone is different when starting out, so just go with the flow. When starting out, twenty minutes each day will be enough for your spirit guides to begin to connect with you and give you guidance.

You can also ask for a sign that you have been heard. This will help you trust in the process. Pick something that will resonate with you, such as a song you like or a black or white feather, and then keep an eye out for your sign over the next few days. When you feel that you have become in tune and comfortable with journeying, you can begin some of the other journeys that are mentioned later in the book (see chapter 7).

❋ ❋ ❋

3

SHAMANIC TOOLS
AND
TECHNIQUES

Shamans use a wide variety of tools, including drums, rattles, plants, water, stones, crystals, and fires. Singing also often accompanies shamanic work. The tools an individual shaman uses will vary depending upon what works best for them in their quest to achieve the shift of consciousness they need. This will enable them to receive the information that is being communicated and to direct the healing by whatever means are most effective. It is important to note that all of these methods may differ or change the feel of the shamanic work, and one is not better than another.

Animal Medicine

Some shamans use either bird medicine or another kind of animal medicine in their daily work by calling upon the spirit of the animal while performing ceremonies or rituals, healing, or journeying to other realms. In some cultures, they did this before going to war with other tribes.

Using the feathers, beaks, claws, or other parts of the animal, shamans call upon its energy or power to help them gain visions, insight, or perspective on the bigger picture. The items they choose depend on the natural instincts of the animal. North America is home to quite a few birds, but indigenous shamans from this region have tended to choose crows, ravens, falcons, hummingbirds, owls, and hawks.

Historically, these creatures have often been killed in a ceremonial way to enable the shaman to make a connection to them, and then they were hung upside down from rafters to dry out until they were needed. The shaman would say prayers over the animal as they cut it open to remove the insides—treating it respectfully unites them to the spirit of the animal. Some of the main animals killed in these ceremonies include bears, beavers, buffalo, deer, and coyote. Shamans would keep the skulls, bones, hooves, claws, teeth, fur, and skin to make talismans and ceremonial clothing. Smaller

items would be kept in their medicine bags. They used these things wisely when they needed some guidance, courage, and wisdom when journeying, or by taking on the power of the animal when performing healing rituals.

In the modern world, we can invoke the power of animals by using pictures of them. We could use fake fur or even toy animals to give an impression of the creatures we are tapping into when trying out these rituals. The intention is what makes the ritual work anyway, and it will be even more effective if we call upon our power animal while carrying out shamanic work.

The Shamanic Drum

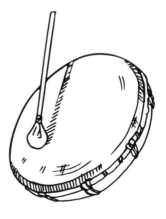

In shamanism, the drum is used for two basic purposes, and one is to shift the state of consciousness. The shaman may wish to move their energy from a normal, daily life condition to a somewhat otherworldly one. When the shaman wants to journey, they need to move into a different state of consciousness, and the rhythmic beating of the drum helps them do that.

The second use for the drum is when the shaman wants to see the patient on a spiritual level—to understand the things that are bothering the person using intuitive or psychic means. The shaman also uses the drum to call their helping and healing spirits forward.

Before buying a drum (or making your own), ask other people who work in this way, or ask your shamanic teacher for advice. Many of the drums used in shamanic work are low pitched, with a strong bass sound. It's worth trying out various drums with different sounds to see whether one seems to work better than others for you.

Some people also like rattles, singing bowls, or other instruments to add to the drumming experience. If you are working alone, without a group to share with, there are albums of journey drumming music available. You can try a few out on YouTube or elsewhere online to see what you like and what works best for you.

Shamanic drums have a particular kind of resonating sound, and there is usually an echo that continues after each beat. In theory, you could use any

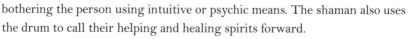

Tip

In my own early days, when I attended group journey sessions, I would try a number of different drums to see which I preferred. I chose a natural-skin drum and then had a similar one made for me. I have to say that I love it, but I don't think the neighbors are too impressed!

drum to journey, but some are harder to handle than others. In shamanic work, you tend to move around with the drum, either to perform healing or because moving around helps you to shift your energy. This means that heavy drums and those meant to be set on the floor are not a good idea because they make it hard for you to move about. This is why many shamanic practitioners use a round drum with a handle directly behind it. I have one of these with a frame made of light wood. Synthetic drums with clunky frames are too heavy and will make your arms tire more quickly.

Traditional drums are made from animal hides, and a good drum maker will source hides in a way that honors the animal. A synthetic drum is made of humanmade materials. There are advantages to each type. Rawhide drums are more sensitive to temperature and humidity, so the drum maker has to tune the drum to what the drummer expects to be a typical environment. If the maker makes the drum too tight and the student takes it to a dry climate, the drum will tighten too much, and it may crack or break; in a humid environment, the drum may become dull or stop working altogether. So choose a product that is suitable to your environment. Drum makers can give you advice on selecting, tuning, and caring for your drum.

Drums tend to come with drumsticks or beaters, and different ones can make different sounds. You might find that a particular drum works better with either a softer or a firmer beater. You can also beat drums with your hand, but some are difficult to handle or require more support.

The most popular synthetic drum is the Remo Buffalo Drum, which according to the company is "inspired by the indigenous cultures of the Americas." Remo is a well-known company that has been making drums for over sixty years. The Buffalo Drum is round, 3.5 inches (9 cm) deep, with the drumhead on one side and the rope handles opposite the head. This drum is not sensitive to humidity and can even be used in the rain.

If you have a synthetic Remo Drum, you can paint it using acrylic paints. Apply a primer before painting, and when the finished design is fully dried, spray a protective coat of clear varnish over it. You will have to reapply this periodically because it will wear off due to the drum being beaten. Natural-skin drums can also be painted, but the porous surface is more of a challenge; your drum maker may be able to give you more information on what to use and the procedure.

Tip

Drum diameters are typically 8 inches (20 cm), 10 inches (25 cm), 14 inches (35 cm), 16 inches (40 cm), and 22 inches (55 cm). The larger the drum, the deeper the sound.

In shamanic belief, everything is alive and has a spirit, and this is also true of the drum. Therefore, one of the things a good drum maker does is to infuse a drum with a good spirit. This works for synthetic drums as well as for natural ones.

It is possible to go on a journey to find the spirit of your new drum, and your power animal or your shamanic teacher can help you if you're new to this.

Connecting to the Spirit of Your Drum

Create a sacred space (see page 47), get comfortable, and close your eyes. Sit with your drum, holding it and getting a feel for it. Let it speak to you. You have to pay attention to your nonvisual senses.

Tip

You can use the same innovation prayer that you use for your drum or for any of your shamanic objects and tools.

Ask your spirit guide to help infuse your energy with the spirit energy of your drum so that you become one with it and form an energetic bond with it. Over time you will become more attuned to your drum, and when you use it, the sound will feel deeper and more vibrational.

You can also use an innovation prayer to connect to your drum by saying, "I call my spirit guide to me to help me to infuse this drum with an energy that's beneficial only to me." Then hold your drum to your heart and imagine your inner light surrounding your drum. Picture being connected to the drum by thin strands of white light.

Repeat this practice for a few days, and during this time, keep your drum someplace where you can see it and touch it often.

Shamanic Drumming

Research done on the shamanic spirit dances has proven what practitioners already knew: that shamanic rhythmic drumming can induce an altered state of consciousness. A rattle, if used in combination with the drum, provides stimulation to higher-frequency pathways in the brain and reinforces the drumbeat by increasing and heightening the overall effect.

The shaman usually starts by beating the drum until they reach a higher state in which they are unable to continue. An assistant then takes over so the shaman's higher state can be maintained. The shaman may start dancing, and the rhythm of the bells and other talismans on their costume will supplement the higher-frequency sounds. Their movements also help to put their nervous system into an altered state. Another element is power songs, which tend to be repetitive and increase in tempo as the shaman reaches the state required to invoke their spiritual guardians and other helpers who will reaffirm their power. They then proceed to contact power animals, animal guides, plants, spirits, and any other entities that will bring forth the information that's required.

The Shaman's Rattle

Rattles are magical tools used to signal the beginning of an important speech or prayer during ceremonies. Shamans also use rattles as tools to communicate with spirit ancestors and to heal patients, during soul retrieval when they need to shake out negative energies, and in dance ceremonies.

Rattles are unique to each culture and may be made of anything, including wood, bone, hair, metal, stone, sinew, and hide. They may have any number of magical items attached, depending on what they are being used for, and may be decorated with paint or other pigments.

Some shamans have three types of rattles: One has a face carved on one side, while the other side is flat and painted with animals or plants. The second is made of wooden hoops with deer hooves or puffin beaks hanging from it. The third has a double head and it's made of wood with intricate carvings on a long stick, to which the shaman would likewise attach puffin beaks. Some shamans choose puffins due to their ability to dive quickly and disappear underwater, which represents the journey to the lower world during a ceremony.

Connecting to Your Rattle

Whether you bought your rattle or made your own with objects you found, you will need to cleanse it. You can do this with salt water or by smudging it (lighting a bunch of dried sage and waving the smoke around the rattle).

Call in your spirit guides and create a sacred space, somewhere in nature if possible, and sit with your rattle for a while, holding it and getting a feel for it. Let it speak to you.

Decide if your rattle is going to be feminine or masculine and what you are going to use it for. Is it for healing, grounding, and clearing? Is it for ceremonies? Or is it a container for spirits? Set your intention and ask your spirit guides to infuse the energy of your intention into your rattle. Energize it in this same way a few more times. Remember to cleanse it often, especially if it is used for healing.

The Shaman's Staff

Modern shamanic practitioners may use a staff as part of their rituals. These can be made of a stick or a branch from a tree that the shaman feels drawn to. They are typically about 2 yards (1.8 m) long and may be decorated with carvings, special symbols, bells, and other items that make sound, or magical objects such as amulets that belong to the shaman. The staff functions as an energy conduit between worlds, and it is used to contact ancestors and spirit helpers for help and guidance with performing ceremonies or healing. During ceremonies, each staff is used to clear negative energy or to shift bad luck.

Making Your Own Staff

It is important to choose your tree wisely when looking for a stick or branch, because it's capable of carrying power. You will need to connect to the tree and ask its permission to take a piece of it. After you have taken the wood, you must remember to give your thanks; you could leave a small offering of food or drink as your sign of gratitude.

Once you have your staff, you need to infuse it with your energy, so use prayer or meditation to connect yourself to it before attaching any sacred items. It is best to craft the items yourself, because that way they will hold a deeper significance to you. You could also attach a large crystal at the top and metal cap at the bottom before you paint it, carve it, or add beads and feathers. You should use whatever works for you and whatever feels right. Once the

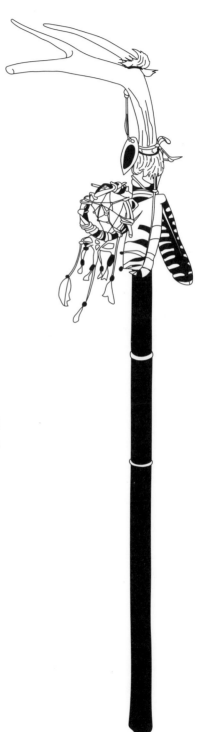

staff is completed, spend some time with it holding it upright. You may feel the energies of the three world levels connecting to it. Pay attention to what happens to your body and the way this makes you feel.

Connecting to Your Staff

Take your staff out with you when you go for a walk. Walk consciously and silently in a relaxed manner.

After a short time, state your intention and ask your spirit guides to help you make an energetic connection between you and your staff. State your intention a few times and keep walking with awareness. Notice how the staff feels. Does it become lighter? Can you feel a change? Has it increased in energy? You may have to do this a few times before you will start to feel the infused vibrational energy that it will absorb from you over time.

The Shaman's Vestment

The vestment a shaman wears plays a big part in the ceremonies and journeys of the shaman. It is a very ancient tradition. There have been images of tribal people from around the world dressed as birds or deer in caves dating back to the Stone Age. Their outfit also provides protection against negative or destructive spirits during a ceremony. A negative spirit cannot effectively attack a shaman wearing their vestment, headdress, or mask nor can it recognize the shaman when they are out of their vestment.

In many traditions from all over the world, the shaman's vestment imitates an animal, such as a deer, bird, or bear, and includes a headdress made of antlers or feathers. In some tribes and cultures, shamans perform ceremonies, with various items attached to a shirt that has a kind of apron at the front and the back that carries representations of snakes, frogs, and other animals. Footwear is also symbolic, with deer hooves, bird claws, or bear paws; leather is rarely used, however. The shaman may hang other items on their clothing during ceremonies and journeys to represent the ritual they performed. Those listed below are used in many kinds of rituals, though they are not generally used for healing.

- Feathers and wings represent astral travel and are for protection.
- Bones and skeletons represent death and rebirth.
- Antlers and horns are used for journeying to connect to the spirits of the animals.
- Human and animal figures represent good or evil spirits.
- Bells are used to frighten away evil spirits.
- Disks represent the sun, the moon, and the entrance to the lower world.
- The sun and moon symbolize the shaman's knowledge of the universe, the influence of other realms, and the planets.
- Chains and ropes are used by the shaman to climb up from the lower world and to come back into their body. These also move around during ceremonies and scare unwanted spirits away.

Dream Catchers

Dream catchers are a tradition among several Native American tribes, though they originated in the Ojibwe tradition. Authentic, traditional dream catchers are handmade from all-natural materials and measure just a few inches across. The hoop is usually constructed of a bent red willow branch covered in stretched sinew and wrapped in leather.

The circular shape of the dream catcher represents the circle of life and death. It also represents the travels of the sun and the moon across the sky. The feathers are meant to keep in good dreams and to allow them to gently descend upon the sleeping person without disturbing them. The strings are meant to symbolize the spider, the web weaver of the natural world. In fact, the Ojibwe word for dream catcher is *asabikeshiinh*, which means "spider."

Some people see spiders as a bit creepy, but for many cultures they are a symbol of protection and comfort. The dream catcher has traditionally been used as a talisman to protect sleeping people, and especially children, from bad dreams and nightmares. It is hung above the bed in a place where the morning sunlight can hit it.

The night air is filled with dreams, both good and bad, and in the Ojibwe culture there are two different ways of understanding how dream catchers work. In the first, the dream catcher attracts and catches all sorts of dreams, allowing the good one to pass through and gently slide down the feathers to comfort the sleeping person below, while the bad dreams are caught up in its protective net and destroyed as they get burned up in the light of day. In the second, good dreams are still caught in the web, but bad dreams escape through the holes.

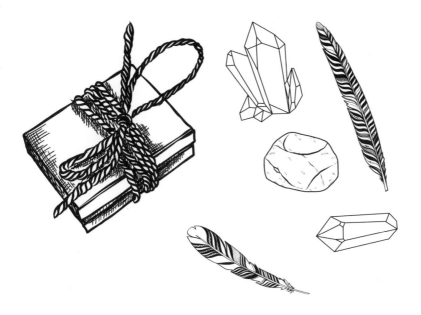

Power Objects

As you go about your daily life, keep an eye open for objects that take your interest; these are power objects. They might be a pebble that you found while walking on an empty beach, a feather that just happened to land in front of you, or a special crystal that you were drawn to or that moved you in some way when you visited a place. Shamans often use a clear quartz crystal (see page 52), which they tend to carry with them at all times. Perhaps you have something that you found and kept from childhood—this could be a power object too.

Shamans typically keep these objects wrapped in animal skin or cloth, but you can keep yours in a box if you wish. These packages are called medicine bundles, and the items are personal because they are not meant to be shown to or talked about with others. When you open the package or box and take out your items, you may realize that one item no longer moves you; if so, return it to the place you found it if possible.

❄ ❄ ❄

POWER ANIMALS

Some people call power animals totem animals, spirit animals, or animal guides, but they all refer to the same concept. Shamans believe that we are all born with an animal spirit guide that will stay with us for the duration of our lifetime. Other guides may come and go along our journey through life, depending on our circumstances and the things we need help with, but our power animal is constant. It is surprisingly easy to find your power animal during a meditation or journey, and this chapter will show you how to see yours in your mind's eye. When we get to know our animal, we can take on their characteristics to aid us with whatever we're dealing with at any given time.

Humans and animals are related, and power animals provide strength to us during our daily life. Shamans can metamorphose into their power animals in order to use their power; and in some cultures, when shamans dance, they wear masks that represent their animal and that evoke their characteristics. The shaman will dance in an increasingly frenzied condition while imitating the actions and cries of the animal.

Tip

Before I started to write this book, I asked my guides to show me my animal, and I have been given a rabbit. This made perfect sense when I looked up the meanings of the rabbit power animal guide. I will go in a bit more detail later in this chapter and tell you more about the most common power animal guides and their meanings.

A Ceremony for Meeting a Power Animal Guide

An animal guide ceremony takes place in a quiet, empty, dimly lit room. The shaman, accompanied by helpers with two rattles and a drum, dances with their eyes half-closed. The ceremony happens in two stages: first the shaman dances in their mind without moving much physically while they or their helpers shake the rattles. Then the shaman will dance with their animal guide, using the drum and reaching for the characteristics and emotions of the animal they are channeling. They will make the noises that the animal guide would make and in some cases will even see the animal manifesting into reality in the room. When the shaman feels they have a good connection, they welcome the animal to enter their body and to stay there for a while. It doesn't matter how aggressive the animal may be; the shaman is in no danger because the power animal is harmless. It is only the spiritual power of the animal, not its physical power, that the shaman needs to use.

A power animal called to help us in healing tends to stay with us for a few years and then they depart, so over the course of a lifetime we will have a number of them. They stay with us, helping us whether we are aware of their presence or not. You can use the meditation on page 73 to meet your power animal.

Once you know your power animal, you should keep track of how you feel on a daily basis. Notice when you feel more powerful, because that is the best time to overcome any major obstacles, and note when you feel dispirited,

Tip

I have noticed that people can look a bit like their power animals, such as having the pointy ears and face of a fox or the strong stance of a bear. I sometimes play a game of trying to work out what animal guide someone has before seeing it or being told what it is.

because you should try to avoid difficult situations during those times. If you feel weak, irritable, or unhappy, don't attempt to help anyone else until you're back to yourself again.

Another interesting point is that during a meditative journey, you may clairvoyantly see a swarm of insects gathering at a particular point on a person or even inside a person's body. This is your own spiritual guide's way of showing you that the person has an illness in that part of the body that needs to be treated. The first port of call for the patient would be to see a conventional doctor and to take the advice and help that is given, but if appropriate, the patient may also come back to the shaman for some spiritual healing.

Finally, whether you are a trainee shaman or just someone who likes to work in a shamanic way, once you've connected with your power animal, you should ask it to be with you whenever you do any kind of spiritual work.

Common Power Animals

Here are some of the more common power animal guides along with brief information on their characteristics and meanings. You may want to buy a dedicated book or research more on power animals if you are interested in more in-depth and comprehensive descriptions of their unique traits.

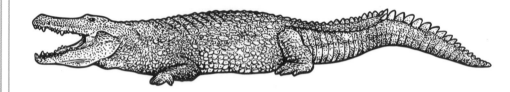

Animal	Characteristics
Alligator	Strong survival instinct; moves silently and unseen; mothering, protection of infants and youngsters
Ant	Industriousness, self-sacrificing, working for the good of the community, teamwork
Badger	Tidiness and organization; rage when cornered; able to communicate with the lower world
Bear	Protective; hidden strength, courage, looking inwards; associated with shamanic rituals and healing, taking care of oneself and one's own needs
Beaver	Expert builders who can rebuild shaky foundations; water elementals who work with the subconscious and therefore are good at finding hidden answers and forgotten dreams
Blackbird	Mysticism; can move between realms with clarity; a messenger
Butterfly	Change, transformation; balance in all things; grace and beauty; renewal, growth; helps one to lighten up

Animal	Characteristics
Cat	Curiosity; exploration of the unknown or the unconscious; courage
Cattle/Cow	Abundance and having enough of what one needs; ability to heal oneself and others; being part of a team
Chicken	Inquisitive, observant, reflective, knowledgeable; independence; protectiveness; able to feel the vibrations of Mother Earth
Cougar	Self-assurance, ability to lead; ability to move unseen; balance; steadfastness; cleverness; awareness; a spiritual warrior
Coyote	Humor, tricks, playfulness, joking, adaptability
Crane	Good fortune; emotional stability; spiritual awakening; ability to restore faith in oneself and one's spirit; rebirth
Crow	Reminds us to look for opportunities to create and make things happen; birds are often messengers, calling us to open up to magic, wisdom, and resourcefulness; speak your truth and do shamanic work
Dog	Faithfulness, loyalty, unconditional love, serving selflessly; forgiveness; teaching
Dolphin	Joy and happiness; harmony; connection to oneself; peace; inner strength
Donkey	Perseverance, strong dedication to spirit; ability to get out of dangerous situations; stubbornness
Dove	Sensitive to emotions; can assist in releasing trauma stored in our cellular memory; love
Dragonfly	Avoidance; tenacity, relentlessness; connection to fairy realms; change, transformation; the spirit world

Animal	Characteristics
Eagle	Sacred messenger; visions from spirit, ability to hear spiritually; ability to heal; ability to see beyond the horizon; courage; strength
Elephant	Teacher of compassion, loyalty, strength, intelligence, good memory; can aid in soul evolution
Ferret	Elusiveness; opportunism; focused power of observation; intuition; sensitivity; can see and know hidden meanings
Flamingo	Power of illusion; shape-shifting; work with group consciousness; clear-sightedness
Fox	Cleverness, cunning; discretion in all things; dream work; shamanic work
Frog	Spiritual cleansing; peace; emotional healing; wisdom; transformation, metamorphosis
Goat	Sure-footedness; can link to past lives; strong foundations; helps to let go of insecurities; independence
Goose	Safely journeys, home protection
Gorilla	Excellent recall; observant nature; loyalty to family; clairaudience; compassion; insight; healing
Hawk or Falcon	Awareness; teller of truths who sees beyond the masks; messenger; ability to move between the realms; prophetic insight, clear vision; awakens our vision and inspires us to a creative purpose
Heron	Balance; has a secure but not fixed inner foundation; clarity of understanding
Hippo	Intuitive knowing; practicality and stability; ability to see beneath the surface

Animal	Characteristics
Horse	Freedom of movement; sure-footedness; ability to overcome adversity; strong emotions; passion
Jaguar	Steadfastness; flexibility; ability to guide others in the lower world; ability to awaken inner sight; power; courage; beauty; strength
Ladybird	Strong family ties; renewal; spiritual idealism; keen instincts; good fortune; changes; true love
Leopard	Power of invisibility; clarity of observation; intuition
Lion	Fearlessness, courage, assertiveness; leadership; gentleness; patience; assertiveness; personal power
Lizard	Ability to let go; elusiveness, ability to avoid enemies
Magpie	Intelligence; adaptability; resourcefulness; ability to live in the light and the dark
Monkey	Good observation skills; clarity; ability to see that which is hidden; unpredictability; power; grace
Moth	Strong healing abilities; ability to perceive with clarity; ability to guide people from the dark to the light
Mouse	Ability to charm; ability to create illusions; family; playfulness
Otter	Bringer of joy and laughter; lightness of touch; medicine for women
Owl	Wisdom; ability to see into shadows; insight; a solo worker but able to assist others when required
Panda	Willpower; ability to connect the seen and unseen; willingness to learn; inner sight; clarity of vision

Animal	Characteristics
Panther	Shape-shifting; invisibility; power of silence; linked to lunar energies
Rabbit	Abundance and wealth; creativity; cleverness; associated with the moon cycle
Rat	Adaptability; self-assurance; sensitivity to the environment; family values; career
Raven	Destroyer; rebuilder; explorer of the unknown; mystery; messenger
Robin	Giver of love and joy; spirit-world messenger
Salmon/Sturgeon	Ability to overcome obstacles; determination; focus; perseverance
Scorpion	Master of self-defense who is always prepared; teaches constant vigilance and how to deal with intensity, whether it is environmental, physical, or spiritual
Seal	Agility; intuition; inner voice; clairaudience
Snake	Rebirth; ability to see the true person; invisibility; guardian of sacred places; keeper of hidden knowledge; power; ability to use earth energies; change
Spider	Weaver of the web of life; ability to interconnect; creativity; busyness; patience; feminine energy
Tiger	Focus; patience; clairvoyance; healing; courage; power; energy; strength and willpower; good use of tactics; prefers working at night; slow and silent approach to problems; devotion and strength; strong connection to full and new moons
Tortoise	Self-reliance; self-determination; focus; inner wisdom; steady progress

Animal	Characteristics
Turtle	Can awaken the senses on the physical and spiritual levels; clairaudience; inner knowledge
Vulture	Adaptability; trust; resourcefulness; innovativeness; seeing the bigger picture
Wolf	Balance; loyalty; independence; a solo worker but able to join others when needed; a teacher of rituals to establish order and harmony; guardian; guide to new paths and new journeys
Woodpecker	Connected to drumming; unique way of doing things and making choices; unique rhythm; change; knowledge; inner strength; mental strength
Zebra	Protector; ability to accept a challenge; ability to use the energy of light and dark to shift realities; hidden knowledge

❋ ❋ ❋

5

SACRED
PLACES

A sacred space is simply a place where you feel safe and secure when practicing your shamanic journeys or performing meditations. It's a place where you will not be disturbed or distracted, and it is a safe place that you can call your own. Don't worry if you don't have a physical space in your home you can dedicate solely to your practices—by creating one in your imagination, you make it real. It doesn't matter whether the place has a physical component or is entirely mental; what is important is that you have one. This will be the first place you will come to in your meditations and for journeying, and it will be the place you visit if you wish to speak to your guides. You may just even want to rest there and use the peace and quiet to reenergize your spirit.

The most common places people tend to think of sacred are either the beach, with the warm sun on your skin and soothing sounds of the ocean waves, or a lush green forest, with high trees, a cool breeze blowing, and the sounds of the birds singing in the distance. If you find, however, that some other imagined scene is more appropriate for you, such as sitting by a roaring fire on a wintery night, by all means, make that your go-to place.

The type of scene is not that important; what matters is that you can imagine every sight, sound, and smell and be able to transport yourself to that place when you need to.

Finding Your Sacred Space

Here is an exercise to help you find your sacred space, which will be of great benefit to you wherever you are on your spiritual path.

Clear your mind and think of your favorite place—a real place or an imaginary one. It may be a place where you like to go and where you can be alone. Picture it in your mind's eye. Think about what is in your special place; visualize the colors and textures.

It may be a beach or a forest, an indoor space or an outdoor one. If it is where you are happy to be, then go with it. Think about the animals you would like to see in this place. Visualize them in your mind's eye and allow them to appear in your space.

Remember this is your own private, sacred space so it can manifest and grow in any way you wish.

Cleansing Energy in Your Space

Shamans often perform cleansing rituals to move, dispel, or change energy by using plants, herbs, crystals, or other implements with the aim of bringing spiritual harmony to a particular space or piece of land. These cleansing rituals can last anywhere between an hour and a day, depending on the size and the energy of the place. Today you can buy ritual kits that contain items such as rose quartz, lavender, sage, salt, essential oils, and palo santo wood. These items are used along with positive intentions or prayer, drumming, singing, and lighting candles.

Shamans have long known of the importance of clearing the energy within a space, and they do this before performing a ritual or ceremony. It's important that you clear your space often, because over time the energy in our homes can become negative or stuck, and this can then have an effect on the people who live in the space. Therefore, keeping the energy clear benefits everyone.

If you move into a new home, it's a good idea to clear the house and perform a ceremony or ritual yourself before you move in. In particular, if you're moving into an old building, it will have had many people living there over the years, with each one bringing their own energy or vibration to the space. There may have been someone who was spiritually ill, and this will leave a residual energy that can affect those who come after. There may also be spirit present if someone has died in the home, and they may be stuck here on earth, missing the opportunity to pass on. If this is the case, it is best to find a medium who can work on the place to move the spirit out of our world and into the light of the "other side." This is also another form of space or energy clearing.

Business premises can have residual energy too, so if you find that things are not going to plan and you seem to be having one setback after another, it might be a good idea to perform a clearing ceremony or find someone to do it for you. It is very unlikely that any medium or space clearer would charge for this service, but it is courteous to at least reimburse the cost of travel. If there is to be an in-depth ceremony or clearing

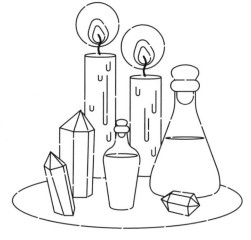

ritual, it is possible that the shaman will charge for this, and the charge depends on the size of the property and how long the job will take.

Here is a list of things that you can do for yourself on a regular basis to keep your space clear:

- Keep all the rooms clean and tidy. Vacuum and dust often; clear away clutter or get rid of it.
- Whenever possible, open all the windows and let the air blow through.
- Burn sage or scented candles, or use aromatherapy oils.
- Play music. The vibrations will uplift everyone and move the energy within the space.
- Add flowers, plants, and crystals to your space.
- Keep a pet. Pets can circulate energy on a lower level just by moving around.
- Move furniture around. By changing the layout, you change the feel of the room.

If you want to go all out, walk around with the intention of clearing the space while calling in your guides and helpers to assist you in your own ritual. It doesn't have to be anything elaborate; just walking around with a sage stick and wafting it into all the corners up high and low will often do. Once you have used the sage in every room, leave it for half an hour, then open all the windows and doors to let the negative energy and the smell out.

Tip

I have a few objects that I use to cleanse my space, including a collection of crystals, stones, shells, and feathers. Sometimes I use herbs, such as sage, or shamanic cards or illustrations of power animals. It depends on what I'm doing. If I don't have what I think I need, I go out to the woods, and I usually find something that piques my interest.

❊ ❊ ❊

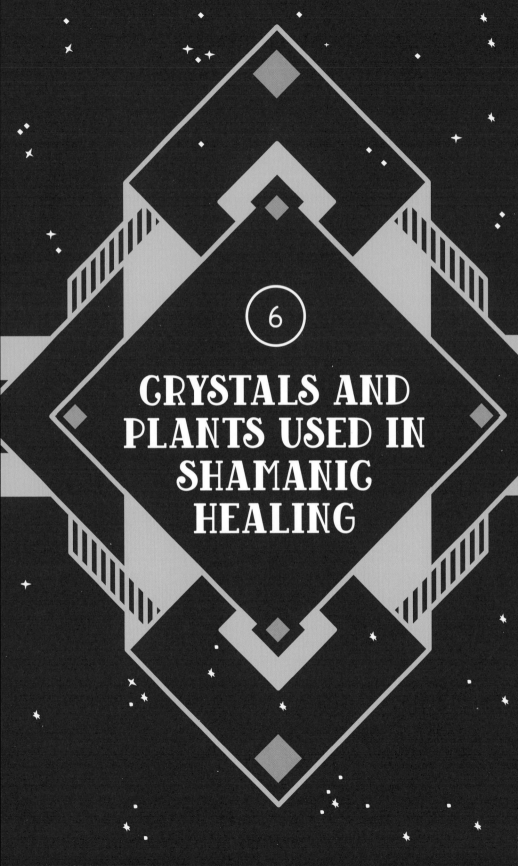

6

CRYSTALS AND PLANTS USED IN SHAMANIC HEALING

For thousands of years, crystals have been used in spiritual practices, in shamanic rituals, and for healing. The use of crystals dates way back, over 6,000 years, to the ancient Sumerians in Mesopotamia. Since then, crystals have been sourced and used in many ancient cultures, such as those found in South America, Egypt, China, Italy, and Greece.

Crystals Used in Shamanism

Shamans often work with crystals, particularly quartz crystals, which are important parts of the medicine bundle and used in very powerful healing practices.

Crystals act as amplifiers that focus, store, and transmit energy and thoughts. They help us to connect to the spiritual realms, psychic dimensions, and altered states of consciousness. They can transform thoughts and energy through vibrations and transmit information we receive from higher beings, guides, and power animals.

If you buy crystals, don't keep them jumbled together, as their energies will become blended; they may even lose power and have to be cleansed and recharged. Only buy what you need, and keep each crystal separate.

I have a set of crystals, including a rose quartz pendulum that I use for clearing the aura or for moving good energy into the right place and bad energy away from the patient during healing sessions. I have had these crystals for many years and feel a strong connection to them—it's as if my energy combines with the crystals when I'm working with them. I would suggest you choose your crystals carefully; touch them and get a feel for them, and you will soon know if a specific crystal is meant for you.

A Rite to Connect to Your Crystals

Once you have cleansed your crystals, you will want to program them and align them to your intentions. Hold the crystal in your hand in front of you, clear your mind, and focus on it. Concentrate on the specific intention you want to program your crystal with and focus your thoughts directly into the crystal. Be clear and concise, and do this until you are happy that your thoughts and energies have been transmitted into the crystal.

Here are a few examples that you can use to program your crystals:

- Infuse rose quartz with love and healing for yourself.
- Use clear quartz to keep your energy clear and protected.
- Citrine can help keep you focused on your work projects and financial goals.

The Shaman's Crystal

Shamans traditionally keep a clear quartz in their medicine bundle. If you only have one crystal, make it this one. Clear quartz is one of the most versatile of crystals and can do just about everything you need: it focuses and directs energy, especially through the quartz points that clear crystals often have, and can be used for meditation, journeying, healing, and dispelling negative energy.

Quartz has protective properties, so you can wear it close to the body, either in the form of jewelry or in a pocket, where it will protect you. You can also place crystals around the home to protect the property. Clear quartz can be used in rituals, sewn into ritual robes, or attached to magical tools. It helps channel energy for healing and is used to keep negativity out and to enhance the safety of the healer as well as the person whom they are healing. During healing, the quartz can be moved over the body, which helps to heal any weak areas in the aura and restores energy.

When using quartz to heal yourself or others, remember to cleanse your stones after using them, because they will pick up any residue of negativity clinging to the aura. You need to cleanse your crystals often, and there are many ways to cleanse and charge them. Many shamans leave their crystals out at night to catch the moonlight, which you can do at any time rather than waiting for the full moon to come into view. You can run them under cold tap water, although clean rainwater is better. You can even bury them in the earth. Another simple method is to leave your crystals outside during the day to charge in the sunlight.

You can also use a crystal as an aid for shamanic dreams by putting it under your pillow or holding it in your hand during journeying. Either way, the quartz can help you to have dreams or visions of a prophetic nature.

Crystal Healing

Crystal healing brings light to the patient's energy field, clears blockages, and rids the individual of feelings of anger, negativity, or even past issues relating to their ancestors or past-life traumas.

You can use crystals as part of your spiritual journey during your meditations or journeying by either placing them on your own body in the areas that you feel need to be cleared or holding them in your hands to connect to their energy for insight. They can also help you keep your chakras clear (see more on page 55).

Choose crystals that have properties corresponding to your intention. For example, let's say you need more motivation; try using carnelian or red jasper. Or if it's more abundance or prosperity that's needed, then jade or citrine is a good choice. For general healing or clearing negativity, you can use clear or smoky quartz. If you are not sure which crystals to use, let your intuition guide you to the right one.

When you're ready, make yourself comfortable someplace where you will not be disturbed. Write out your intention and place it in front of you, then put your crystals on top

Tip

••••◆◆◆◆◆◆•••••

I have used shamanic crystal healing to clear past-life issues that are giving a patient phobias or emotions that they cannot understand. It helps them break away from old relationships that they need to leave in the past or to deal with the emotional residue left from family issues. It is fascinating at times to see what is revealed and to see how, once the patient can understand where these feelings or emotions stem from, they can start their own internal healing process.

of your written intention. Now place your hand on top of the crystal and close your eyes. Visualize a ray of white light energy from the universe coming down into your crown chakra and focus that energy through you and out of your hand into the crystal. Imagine this light surrounding your crystal and your intention. Do this for a few minutes, then when you feel ready, open your eyes. To feel more connected to your crystal, you may want to carry it around in your pocket or sit holding it while you relax for a few days.

Crystal Protection

If you have a relative, neighbor, work colleague, or boss who is subject to fits of anger, you know how unsettling this is, and you may even find yourself feeling irritable and angry just by being around the person when they are in a bad mood. Indeed, it is hard for anyone not to feel upset or angry when someone around them is raging out, to the point where even those who have no interest in spiritual matters whatsoever and who are as emotionally aware as a pile of bricks will feel unnerved. (More on these "power intrusions" in the next chapter.)

To soften bad vibes from others, there are a few protection crystals you can use. Black tourmaline or clear quartz can be placed in the corners of your property to create a protective grid for dealing with problematic neighbors. You could also place rhodonite in your doorway, as this crystal is one of the best for new beginnings. Even if you've had some bad problems with colleagues or family members in the recent past, this may help you smooth things over and move forward in a positive way. You could also try wearing or putting a small crystal in your pocket.

Chakras

Chakras are swirling wheels of energy that correspond to massive nerve centers in the body. While the term "chakras" comes from the Vedic tradition from Indian, similar ideas have long been understood by shamans around the world. All of the seven main chakras contain bundles of nerves and major organs and are key to our psychological, emotional, and spiritual states of being. Since everything is moving, it's essential that our seven main chakras stay open and remain aligned and fluid. If there is a blockage, their energy cannot flow.

Keeping a chakra functioning properly is a bit of a challenge, but it isn't too difficult for those who develop awareness. Since mind, body, and spirit are intimately connected, awareness of an imbalance in one area will help bring the others back into balance.

You may notice things happening to you when you start to clear your chakras; for instance, you may find yourself crying or coughing. This is part of the cleansing process, and it shows that you are allowing your emotions and energies to flow. Going outdoors and into the world of nature can be a good way to heal yourself, so you may choose to take a walk in the country, or you may feel the need to be near water. Listening to healing music is also beneficial, as is going to someone who can give you a gong sound bath, because the tones and vibrations of the gong correspond to certain chakras and therefore can help them to clear and heal.

Listed here are the main chakra points, where on the body they are located, and the colors that are linked to them. Try to choose crystals that are of the same color as the chakra you are trying to heal. If you don't have the right crystals, you can always use a clear quartz, which stands in for any color and which can be used for any purpose.

• The root chakra is situated at the base of the spine. The color associated is red.

 • The sacral chakra is situated at the navel. The color associated is orange.

 • The solar plexus chakra is situated just under the rib cage. The color associated is yellow.

 • The heart chakra is situated in the center of the chest. The color associated is green.

 • The throat chakra is situated in the neck area. The color associated is blue.

 • The third-eye chakra is in the middle of the forehead. The color associated is purple.

 • The crown chakra is situated at the top of the head. The color associated is white.

Tip

Different practitioners use the chakra colors in slightly different ways. For instance, some consider the third-eye chakra to be dark blue and the crown chakra purple, but others use the colors in the same way that I do.

Performing Chakra Healing

To heal someone's chakras, lay them down in a comfortable place, maybe on a blanket on the ground, and place the crystals beside the body in line with the chakras. You can select crystals that link with the color of the chakras or those that have special abilities, such as red crystals to energize a sluggish or blocked chakra, or blue ones that can calm an overactive chakra and help the patient to communicate more successfully. The crystals work with the energy of the body you, so focus on the areas one by one. Imagine the crystals working and clearing blockages. Relax into the healing and let the crystals do their work. When you feel the work is done, have the person sit up slowly and offer them water.

A Centering Chakra Meditation

If you want to do some healing and feel more relaxed, doing a root and sacral chakra meditation can often help. During this simple but effective meditation, you will focus on specific areas of the body one at a time.

Sit with your shoulders back and your spine straight. Try to relax all your muscles as you close your eyes and breathe deeply. Inhale through the nose and exhale through the mouth.

Turn your focus to the area of the root chakra, which is situated right below your tailbone. Take notice of any tightness or stiffness in the area.

The root chakra is associated with the color red; try picturing a red glow at the base of your spine, then slowly expand it, making the whole area warm and relaxed. Relax into this sensation for a few minutes.

Then move your attention up toward the sacral chakra, which is situated about 3 inches (7.5 cm) below the navel and at the center of your lower belly. Again take notice of how the area feels.

The sacral chakra is associated with the color orange; picture an orange glow around your navel and expand it until you feel more relaxed.

When you feel ready, slowly open your eyes. Repeat the following affirmation to yourself a few times: "I am stable, grounded, and relaxed in this moment." Sit quietly for a few minutes as your awareness comes back into the room.

Plants Used in Shamanism

Plants are used in shamanism in a way that will honor the plant spirit, so the tradition is to prepare them with a particular intention and to do so in a ceremonial space. Taking plant medicine is often accompanied by the shaman singing or chanting, drumming, and shaking rattles. These plant ceremonies usually take place in darkness, around a fire or in a lodge, and they  often last all night. The idea is to obtain visions, cure illness, or connect with spirits and guides. Sometimes the shaman works along with others who sit in a circle around him and each person has an individual experience.

Warning Descriptions here show what traditionally trained shamans do, but you mustn't do any of this yourself. The best way to use plants is to put them on an altar and then sing, dance, and shake rattles. *Never* eat any of them and *never* make any of them into a drink and then swallow mixtures made from plants that you have collected. *Never* give plants to other people whom you think may try to eat or drink them. The altar is the right place for these things, and when you have finished working with them, you should either bury them or put them on a bonfire.

Plant ceremonies have become more popular with group retreats, but some people will have frightening experiences, especially if they have suffered a lot of emotional and mental stress throughout their lives. However, many people have

Tip

Some practices use purgative drugs to rid a person of bad spirits or vibes and to cleanse the person's system, but I *do not* recommend this at all. If you are looking for healing, the best thing to do is visit a shamanic healer and have some healing in a safe environment without doing anything that could be harmful. It is amazing what a visit to a decent healer can achieve—and all without putting your health at risk.

a positive outcome because they gain insight and healing. Nothing can prepare you for the experience because everyone is different, and it really does depend on each person's emotional and mental state at the time. Those who have gone through this ceremony many times and have cleared and healed themselves will eventually experience more spiritual enlightenment and insight.

Plant Helpers

Shamans use the power offered by not only animals and other guides but also plants. Over the years a shaman will accumulate many helpers, although plant helpers tend not to have as much power as spirit animals.

Unless you are particularly interested in plants, you probably won't know what the wild plants are that you see growing in the hedgerows and woods, so if a plant seems to attract you, sit down with it and become familiar with its details. You could take a piece home and look it up in a book or online, but remember to seek the plant's permission before you pick it, explaining your intention to use it within your work. It might actually be a better idea to use your smartphone to take a photo of the plant and then look it up without disturbing it—which is not only more respectful but safer, because you won't necessarily know if the plant happens to be poisonous.

If a plant is not poisonous, you can always come back another time and take a few cuttings. You could

Tip

Not all plants are safe to handle because some are poisonous and can cause injury and harm, so be sure you've accurately identified any plant before touching it. You can download a plant-identification app on your smartphone or buy a plant book to take it with you to check out the plants that you see in the wild before you even touch them.

even use your developing clairvoyant power to help you locate more of the same kind of plant. Take time to study your plant; if you see something weird happening, such as the plant changing shape in front of your eyes, hold it in your hand and ask it to become your plant helper.

Shamanic Oils

Shamans believe in the healing wisdom of magical oils and have long used scented oils to make incense, ointments, tinctures, and charms. These sacred oils are made by heating fragrant plant matter, leaves, flowers, and bark in carrier oils made from olives, sesame seeds, and other sources. Some of the earliest fragrant oils made in this way were frankincense, myrrh, and cinnamon oils, and these classic scents are still in use by modern shamans.

Infused oils offer many health benefits and can be used by breathing in their aromas or applying them directly on the soles of the feet and the palms of the hands. These are highly absorptive areas of our bodies, so they are an excellent way for essential oils to enter our systems. Shamans also believe that our hearts reach out to others through the palms. A gentle hand or foot massage can balance the nervous system and change the way we feel in minutes, so it is a wonderful way to help others when used in healing. Even therapists who don't follow shamanic traditions use essential oils in aromatherapy.

While they are normally used for healing purposes, oils have their magical uses too. When used with the right intentions, they can change a person's luck, improve their love life, bring success, and promote more energy.

Plant-derived scented oils contain the magical energies of the plants from which they are made—they are the trees, shrubs, and flowers in liquid form. Plants are living entities with their own living intelligence that works in perfect harmony with nature. Some plants have magical properties, which are highly concentrated in the form of essential oils. Synthetic fragrance oils may smell quite similar to the real thing, but they won't have the same natural ingredients contained in botanical oils or the spirit of the plant within them.

Natural magical oils have the power to put us in a happier or more relaxed mood. The mixed scents of myrrh and cedarwood, or lavender and clove, instantly awaken something in us that goes beyond our ordinary sense of smell. These aromas put us into a different frame of mind and, when used in magic, rituals, meditation, or journeying, can help to put us more in touch with the spiritual realms. It is said that using botanical oils can provide a direct link between the natural physical world and the spiritual plane.

Here are a few examples of oil mixtures that you might like to try, especially if you are new to using oils or don't know where to start. When choosing your oils, just go with your instincts and pick those that you are drawn to or like to smell. Notice how the scent of the oil makes you feel. Make sure to buy from a reputable retailer and to store the oils away from direct sunlight in a box or drawer. You can build up your collection over time and experiment by mixing two oils together in an oil warmer.

Warning Never put undiluted oils directly on your skin—they must be mixed with a base oil or they will cause irritation. The base oil can be olive oil, sunflower oil, coconut oil, palm oil, or whatever you have in your cupboard at home.

Inner Vision Oil

This mixture will enhance spiritual and clairvoyant awareness. Add the following oils to your base oil:

- 4 drops of lemongrass
- 2 drops of bay
- 1 drop of nutmeg

Mix together and put a small amount on the forehead before meditating or journeying.

Inner Peace Oil

Use this mixture when you are nervous or upset, as it will
help to calm you down. Add the following oils to your
base oil:

- 3 drops of lavender
- 3 drops of ylang-ylang
- 2 drops of chamomile
- 1 drop of rose

Mix together and put a small amount on your wrists, palms, and forehead,
then take some time out to still your mind and relax.

Energy Oil

Use this mixture when you're feeling tired, ill, despondent,
or sad, or when you need to strengthen your energy reserves.
Add the following oils to your base oil:

- 4 drops of orange
- 2 drops of lime
- 1 drop of lemon
- 1 drop of cardamom

Mix together and place small amounts on your wrists, your palms, the soles
of your feet, and your temples before going to bed or taking a nap.

Attraction Oil

This will attract love, success, or whatever it is that you want
to draw into your life. Add the following oils to your base oil:

- 7 drops of rose
- 3 drops of lemon
- 1 drop of peppermint
- 1 drop of orange

Mix together and add a small amount to your bathwater.
Light a few candles to set the scene, and think about the things you want to
manifest into your life. After the ritual, write them down in your journal,
if you keep one.

WEATHER SHAMANS

Shamans have for many centuries worked with the weather to help restore and maintain balance and harmony, to heal the earth, and to relieve suffering in the world. They work with spiritual forces and talk to the elements, and they try to influence the weather by performing chants, prayers, dances, and songs and by making offerings during weather ceremonies.

Shamans have a deep understanding of nature and the importance of restoring and healing the planet. They spend many hours building a relationship with the weather spirits, talking with them, and watching the sky. Depending on their culture and their local climate, they may ask for heavy clouds and rain to grow their crops and feed their animals, or they may ask for a dry spell and sunshine.

Even people who are skeptical of shamanic practices often hire weather shamans to perform rituals before important outdoor events, such as fashion shows, celebrity events, and even royal weddings.

You can learn to read the weather by studying the clouds and tuning in to the atmosphere. For example, you can pick up on the stillness that happens just before a storm. Walking in nature and paying attention to the animals and the way they behave can also help, because they can tell when the weather is changing—usually long before most humans pick up on it.

❋ ❋ ❋

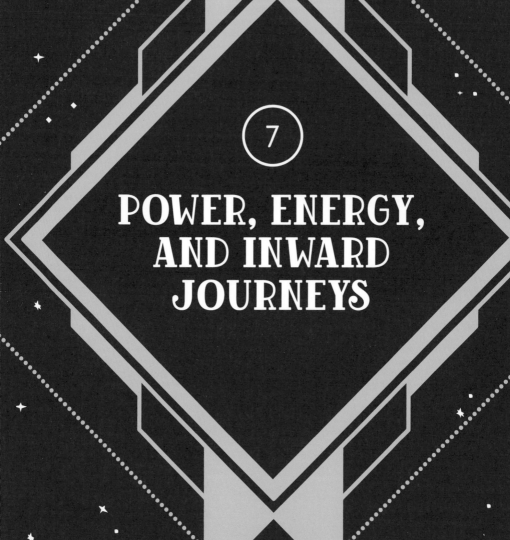

7

POWER, ENERGY, AND INWARD JOURNEYS

Shamans believe that illness is due to power intrusion or loss of power, which manifests as symptoms of pain and discomfort that are often accompanied by an elevated temperature. This is fairly similar to the way in which conventional medicine sees germs and infection.

Power intrusions can occur when we find ourselves around those who are angry or hostile and project that emotion onto others. It is important for shamans to learn to protect themselves from these energies by using their guardian spirit power. Even if you are not a practicing shaman, if you are a spiritually aware person, you may notice energy when someone enters a room or comes in contact with you. Be aware that sometimes it can be our own selves causing the damage, so if you feel that you're angry or upset often, you should take notice of the times, the situation you are in, and the people you are with when it happens. It could be that you are picking up on the energy of others without knowing it and reflecting it back on them. If you feel this happens to you, I suggest that you do a lower journey to find your spirit animal (see page 77) and thereby regain your power. If that doesn't work, you may need to visit a shaman who can extract the unpleasant energy from your aura, your chakras, and your mind.

The shaman will draw these bad vibrations out mentally and psychically, but this can be a difficult and lengthy process, and they must call upon their spirit helpers to help them.

I use my hands to pull and dislodge energy by working on the troublesome area of a patient in this situation; it often feels either warm or cold to my palms while I run my hands a few inches above their body. Sometimes when I feel that there's a lot of work to be done, I have used an egg to absorb the negative energy, rolling it over the area. After the session, I either bury the egg or flush it away down the toilet.

Tip

I must stress the point that it isn't necessary to touch a person when working with them. Although in some cases it can be beneficial, no shaman should touch their patient without prior permission.

The Empath Experience

Many people will feel unsettled if a place has a bad atmosphere, or if it doesn't "feel right," without them being able to explain exactly why this is. In fact, this is such a common phenomenon that it is accepted by virtually everyone, regardless of whether they are into spiritual matters or not. However, some individuals are born with that extra layer of sensitivity that makes them an empath, or what is known in the spiritual world as a "psychic sponge." An especially sensitive empath may find it hard to know whether the feelings they are experiencing are their own or not!

Some people are fully aware of their empathic powers from a young age, but others find themselves becoming more sensitive and empathetic as a result of spiritual training. For both groups of people, protection is always useful. We are all surrounded by a force field that is called the aura, but it isn't always as strong as it needs to be, so a quick fix will be necessary. If you're an empath who finds yourself among difficult people, you can use aura-strengthening techniques, such as imagining yourself in a suit of armor, a shiny egg, or some other reflective material. You may shut your chakras quickly and imagine doors or gates in front of your more vulnerable ones. Some will call on their spiritual guides for protection. Among shamanic traditions of various cultures, some techniques are similar to one another and some are unique. Some can be done instantly, such as calling on one's totem animal, and others take time, such as soul retrieval.

Inward Journeys

Journeying inward is essential to maintaining your power, protecting yourself from the energies of others, and spiritual health healing. It is a good idea to record the instructions for the journeys as it would be very difficult to remember each step just by reading them. These journeys will help you meet your ancestors and find your spiritual guides and also your power animals. Remember that these animals are often also referred to as spirit animals, totem animals or animal guides.

If you are a bit more advanced, you can also listen to recorded drumming during the meditation. Always do the following grounding and protection attunement, as this will prevent you from becoming light-headed and "spacey," and it will protect you from the highly unlikely event of some unwanted spiritual force trying to interfere. Do this before your journey into the spiritual realms, and make sure that you close down again afterward.

Grounding and Protection

The easiest way to ground and protect yourself is to imagine yourself enclosed in a bubble or a dome of white light. Visualize it starting at the top of your head and surrounding your body all the way down until it reaches the ground. As you do this, ask your spirit guides for protection.

When you finish any meditation, visualize yourself "closing down." A simple way to do this is by running your hand across the top of your head and asking your guides to help. When I'm not working, I keep myself closed because if I opened up to all the energies or vibrations around me, I would feel constantly worn out. You can tell when you're not closed down properly, as you will start to feel drained and, in some cases, even light-headed or "spacey."

When you have finished closing, remember to thank your guides for helping you, connecting with you, and protecting you. Then, get up and walk around and drink some water or eat something light. After doing this several times, you will start to recognize what it feels like to open and close your energy channels.

A Meditation Journey to Meet Your Ancestors

Some cultures believe that their dead relatives and ancestors can be accessed during trances or meditative journeys, and that these people can be called upon to advise and help individual people or give advice. It is worth carrying out a journey to meet your ancestors to ask them to give you strength and wisdom.

- Allow yourself to relax. Feel your breathing slow down and become deeper and deeper as you feel more relaxed. Become aware of your heartbeat slowing down.
- Relax your arms and legs. Then, slowly, relax the rest of your body. Enjoy the feeling of relaxation for a few minutes.
- Take yourself to your sacred place, the place in your mind that allows you to feel safe.
- Imagine that you are walking along. Suddenly, you feel the urge to turn around. Behind you is a door. It's a heavy, old oak door with images carved on it. It has a big metal lock and handle. Visualize a key.

- Take your key and open the door. As it slowly opens, you will see a pathway, and soon you will notice your spirit guide is waiting to accompany you. Step onto the path and walk together.
- Above you is a canopy of trees; flowers and herbs line the path. Take notice of what animals besides your animal guide that you see around you. Notice all you can as you follow the path. See the colors and smell the aroma of the plants and wildlife. Notice how the path feels under your feet and the smells of the herbs as you walk on them. There's a warm gentle breeze against your skin.
- The path curves to the right, where it leads out of the trees. There in front of you is a rainbow-colored bridge made of light. See how it shimmers and glistens. See how beautiful it is.
- Cross the bridge. As you reach the other side, come to a stop.
- You see an old brass bell hanging from a wooden frame. It is big and heavy, and hanging from a string beside it is a brass hammer.
- Take the hammer and strike the bell three times, calling for an ancestor to come and teach you what they know. The sound is clear, and it echoes all around you, the noise hanging in the air and vibrating.
- Just before the sound finally dies away, a figure appears in the distance. It comes slowly toward you.
- As the figure come into view, notice what they are wearing. It may be garments from times gone by, or it may be modern clothes. Perhaps the figure is wearing some kind of robes. Let your mind's eye show you what they look like. Notice the strength and power that shimmers about them.

- The figure stops in front of you. As you see them up close, you realize that it's yourself from a previous life. Greet yourself.
- Your ancestor leads you to an area beside the bridge. You have questions you need to ask, and they have knowledge to impart to you. Ask for their wisdom and knowledge.
- Take some time to rest here with your ancestor. Know that you will understand the importance of what you have learned from them when the time is right. Some of it will sink in deep into your memory and you will use it without being aware of it. For now just be still and listen.
- When you feel ready, thank your ancestor, return to the bridge, where your animal guide is waiting for you. Follow them back across the bridge.
- When you get to the other side, you may stop for one last look over the rainbow bridge, but you will see that your ancestor has gone. However, know that they will be there with you if you need them and that they have shared their strength and power with you.
- As you follow the path back the way you came, notice that a fog has sprung up. Continue to follow your animal guide; you know that you will be led back safely.
- Notice that you feel lighter than usual, and your aches and pains all seem easier.
- Follow the path back through the woods until you reach the oak door.
- Hug your guide. Ruffle the hair on your spirit animal's head if you wish. Say goodbye for now and watch them return to the woods, knowing that they will be with you whenever you need them.

- Turn and walk through the door, back to your sacred place. Feel deep within you that you will remember what your ancestors have shown you and that the knowledge will come to your aid when you need it.
- Allow yourself to become aware of your physical body and bring your focus back to earth. Concentrate on your breathing.
- When you are ready, open your eyes.
- Take a moment to sit or lie quietly and get your bearings back. Have some water, then when you are ready, write up any notes you want to remember. Don't forget to ground yourself.

A Meditation Journey to Meet Your Spirit Guides

All forms of spirituality share a belief in spiritual guidance, and the belief systems that do not follow a standardized religious practice usually believe in various kinds of spiritual guides. Some people have their spiritual guides "on-line" so to speak, and know how to connect with them very quickly, while others struggle with this until they and their guides get accustomed to the process, after which it gets easier. This meditation will enable you to meet and become more familiar with your main spirit guide.

- Allow yourself to relax. Feel your breathing slow down and become deeper and deeper as you feel more relaxed. Become aware of your heartbeat slowing down.
- Relax your arms and legs. Then, slowly, relax the rest of your body. Enjoy the feeling of relaxation for a few minutes.
- Take yourself to your sacred place, the place in your mind that allows you to feel safe.
- Visualize yourself walking along a path. As you bring your path into focus in your mind's eye, see in the distance a deep, lush green forest. As you walk along this path, notice the silence and the peacefulness while you wander among the trees, looking at the plants and the flowers. Notice how the gentle, subtle breeze causes the leaves of trees and plants to sway and dance.
- You can hear your own footsteps as you enjoy the pleasant walk, fully immersing yourself into your senses.
- After some time, you hear the distant sound of flowing water. As you walk farther along the path, it brings you closer to the sound.
- You come upon a huge clearing. The sun is shining right down into the clearing, illuminating a stone bridge ahead of you. Below the bridge, you see gently flowing water with the sunshine shimmering on the surface. The water is clear and blue. The bridge is wide, and you will have plenty of room to cross.
- Looking toward the other end of the bridge, you see some steps that lead up to a stone archway that is completely covered in beautiful green vines and leaves. On each side of the archway is a stone wall also covered in beautiful green vines and leaves. Whatever is beyond the archway is not yet known to you, for you cannot see that far ahead.
- Walk across the stone bridge toward the archway. As you do, you feel a distinct sensation of peace overcoming you. With each step, you feel

your old physical life fading further and further away, as if it were a distant memory. You feel you have come a long way, yet time has no meaning here, and it does not concern you.

- As you climb the steps that lead to the archway, you become aware that the view beyond the arch is somehow distorted. You feel a sense of beckoning love and familiar belonging ahead of you.
- Step through the arch. Suddenly all your surroundings change, and you sense warmth that engulfs you like a loving blanket.
- You now find yourself on a path completely covered in flower petals. On each side of the path is a long hedge made from hundreds and hundreds of flowers of all descriptions. It is the most beautiful display of color and nature you have ever seen.
- There is a magical fragrance that captivates you as the flowers seem to come alive with your presence. The two hedges direct you down the path.
- Soon you begin to make out a structure ahead.
- As you come closer, you see that it is your dream cottage, your soul's sanctuary. It is your special sacred home away from home. It is your special secret place.
- Enter the cottage. Once inside, allow your mind's eye to show you your surroundings. You find everything you hold of value here—everything you have ever had or ever wanted. The architecture is as you wish, as are the ornaments and the furnishings.
- Make your way into the main living space—you are expecting a guest any time now. Take a seat in the place that is waiting for you. Prepare the room as you wish, ready for your spirit guide's arrival.

- No one can enter your sacred cottage without your permission. You are completely safe and at peace here. Invite your spirit guide to join you. While you wait, reflect on any questions you may wish to ask them.
- Silently and gracefully, your spirit guide enters the room, appearing to you in a form you feel comfortable with. The guide's presence radiates complete unconditional love, compassion, and wisdom.
- Your spirit guide speaks first, telling you their name. They hold a gift for you, which they place in your hands. This gift can be anything, but it will be personal and significant to you.
- Thank your guide for their gift and invite them to sit with you. Now is your opportunity to ask any questions you may have. Spend as much time as you need, and exchange all that you feel you need to.
- When you have finished your conversation, thank your spirit guide for coming and for their advice and comfort. They will leave the room as silently and gracefully as they entered.
- You feel spiritually empowered, full of joy and gratitude. When you are ready to leave, remember to take your gift with you.
- Make your way out of your cottage and back along the path of flowers.
- When you reach the archway, pass through it. Descend the steps and walk back across the bridge.

- Follow your way back along the path through the lush green forest until it leads you back to your sacred space.
- Allow yourself to become aware of your physical body and bring your focus back to earth. Concentrate on your breathing.
- When you are ready, open your eyes.
- Write down everything you remember. Record your spirit guide's name, what they looked like, the gift you received, and everything else you saw, felt, and heard. Have some water, and don't forget to ground yourself.

A Meditation Journey to Meet Your Power Animal

Power animals are central to Native American spirituality. Some Native Americans believe that these may be reincarnated human souls, while others see them as animals whose traits can be tapped into to give you the strength, agility, mental acuity, and courage that you may need to cope with life. It is important to meet your particular power animal, as it came into this life with you at birth and it will be with you for life, which means that you can access it whenever you need its wisdom and help to guide you. You also have power animals that come and go as you need them over the course of your life. This meditation will introduce you to one or more of your power animals.

- Allow yourself to relax. Feel your breathing slow down and become deeper and deeper as you feel more relaxed. Become aware of your heartbeat slowing down.
- Relax your arms and legs. Then, slowly, relax the rest of your body. Enjoy the feeling of relaxation for a few minutes.
- Take yourself to your sacred place, the place in your mind that allows you to feel safe.
- Now, follow a path that leads you to a large cave. As you enter the cave, you look around and you see rugs and skins on the floor, carvings etched onto the walls. Everything is in neutral colors. There are makeshift shelves on the walls with various books, pots, and many other items for you to look at. You notice that there are dried herbs and flowers hanging from the ceiling, and their musky and aromatic scents fill the cave. In the dim light, the oil burners send shadows around the walls.
- You know you are safe here.
- Move to the mouth of the cave. You can hear the sound of rushing water, and sunlight is spreading its warmth as you step outside.

- You discover that you are on a ledge high above the sea. Waves are crashing on the rocks below and throwing sprays of water high into the air, coating the ledge with droplets. As you examine the ledge, you see that there is a path curving downward through the rocks.
- Follow this path downward. The crashing waves hit the rock wall, and you can feel the vibrations and power of it through your feet as you descend onto the shore.
- The waves break against the cliff, then retreat once again. The rhythm is steady and relaxing. The fine, misty sea spray is cool against your skin.
- There is a path leading away from the beach. Follow it.
- Now find yourself among oak trees and surrounded by flowers and wild herbs. These form a blanket of color beneath the gently nodding branches.
- As you walk through the trees, the sound of the waves starts to diminish. Soon the sea sound is barely a murmur in the background. All you can hear are the birds and crickets and other wonderful creatures around you.
- Herbs and grasses scrunch against your feet, wafting up their aromatic scents.
- Soon the path you are on opens up and joins a larger path. Stop here and leave a little sign so that you can find your way back later—perhaps a few stones at the side of the path as a marker.
- Follow the new path until you come to a clearing. In the center stands a huge old oak tree. It towers over the other trees, and its massive roots spread out across the floor. It is the oldest and biggest tree—the world tree.
- As you get closer, you see a figure. Dressed in green and brown, he almost blends into his surroundings as he sits on an enormous lower branch of the huge tree. You hear sounds of music, like that of a flute, and you realize that it is he who is playing.
- As you approach, the figure puts the instrument down.
- You see that what you thought were merely shadows above his head are horns, and you suddenly notice that his legs are those of a goat. His eyes are old and mischievous, and he regards you with a blank expression, waiting.
- You realize this is Pan, the god of the wild, keeper and protector of the animals, and you need to ask his permission to meet your power animal. He just sits and watches you with a twinkle in his eye, as he sees you have recognized him. Now ask him in your own words to allow you to meet your power animal.

- Pan listens. He seems to stare deep into your soul. Then he takes a horn hanging on the tree behind him and blows it three times, making deep, clear sounds that resonate through the air.
- Suddenly, from the other side of the tree comes your power animal. You greet the animal and then look up and thank Pan.
- You walk back toward the path with your power animal beside you. Feeling happy and somehow more complete, soon you arrive back at the marker you left for yourself.
- Your power animal leads you along the path. You watch and admire how it moves and watch the power and grace of it. The bond between you is growing all the time, and you feel as though you are with an old friend.
- As you walk together, allow yourself to slip into a quiet contemplation. Share this contemplation with your trusted friend. Ask any questions that come to you.
- Soon you hear sounds of the sea—you have reached the beach. The coolness of the breeze and the spray is refreshing. Your animal leads you back up the path by the cliff.

- As you return to the cave, you see that a fire has been set for you. Its warmth and flames are a welcome sight, and you sit down near it.
- Thank your animal for bringing you back. You may stroke or hug it if you wish.
- From now on, your power animal will share its wisdom and strengths with you. Give it permission to share your life and your journey. You can now spend as much time as you need, asking questions, knowing that it will walk in your shadow keeping you safe, guiding and guarding you. Be aware of the lessons it can teach you. Follow its lead and enjoy its company.
- When you are ready to return to your sacred space, allow yourself to become aware of your body, and bring your focus back. Concentrate on your breathing.
- When you are ready to do so, open your eyes.
- Write down the animal you saw and a description of what it looked like. Consult pages 40 to 45 for some introductory information on what your particular power animal may mean. Have some water, and don't forget to ground yourself.

A Note on Guardian Spirit Journeys

One of the interesting things about guardian spirit journeys I have noticed in my work is that there are a lot of coincidences. For instance, once a patient has been reunited with their power animal and finds out what that animal is, it is common for them to feel that they already have a strange connection to that type of animal. The patient may also feel the things the shaman felt and see the things they saw before the shaman ever explains what happened. This is often more noticeable if the journey is performed in a group, as several members of the group may experience the presence of the same animal. This is a good thing, because it shows that the animal guide that has been returned to the patient is working. In some Native American tribes, members don't tell others about their power animal, as that is said to cause it to lose its power. But those who take their journeys in groups can talk about the animal, as in this case it doesn't lead to power loss.

The Spirit Canoe Journey

This is a long journey that involves several shamans and a large group. The purpose is to help or heal someone who is in trouble because their power animal has left them and needs to be brought back. The group joins together to make a journey to the lower world using the spirit canoe method. The shamans then stand in two lines to represent an imaginary canoe inside a large house. Traditionally, each shaman lays a magical cedar board on the dirt floor between the two rows. Each board is decorated with the shaman's own  choice of images, usually a depiction of their own first vision of a spirit canoe.

Each shaman holds a pole of about 6 feet (2 m) long, which they use to paddle or pull the imaginary canoe along. This is accompanied by shaking rattles, beating drums, and singing. As each person present mentally descends into the water to start their journey into the lower world, they sing a spirit guardian song. Sometimes this journey can last as long as four or five nights, with the group sleeping during the day and starting again at night. It usually takes two nights to descend into the lower world in order to retrieve the lost guardian animal for the person they are trying to help. As soon as they have located the animal, another two shamans will take charge of the return journey and place the power animal back with or even into the person. They end the ceremony by dancing.

8

SHAMANIC DREAMS

Shamans believe in dreams. There are three types of dreams: the "ordinary" kind and the kind of big dream that repeats over a few nights. The other type is very important. It is a very vivid kind of dream that makes the dreamer feel as though he is awake. These dreams are said to be communicated by a guardian spirit or power animal, and sometimes the animals will even appear in the dream.

Big dreams are messages, but you shouldn't analyze them for hidden meanings or messages. For example, let's say you had a dream in which you had a car accident. Rather than interpreting this as some kind of metaphor, you should take this as a warning that the accident may happen—and by being forewarned, you may be able to change the outcome. One way to influence events is to reenact the dream with the help of a friend who acts as a temporary shaman for you. Begin by acting out the dream as you experienced it, but change the ending. Even if you don't do this and the accident still occurs, by being more aware and more careful when driving because you know it's a possibility ahead of time, you may be able to mitigate the damage.

It's common to have a dream about something you are considering doing, but if the outcome doesn't end well in your dream, you would be advised not to undertake whatever it was you were thinking of or planning on doing—or, at the very least, you should change the way you were going to go about it. A shaman understands by this that they are "fully in their power," meaning they have the strength and the ability to shift things around by spiritual means.

Dreamtime

Dreamtime is the altered state shamans enter that allows their soul to leave their bodies, travel to other dimensions, and receive messages from the cosmos and the spirit world. Sometimes when I want information, I ask my guides to put the information I need into a "waking dream"—a dream I will remember after waking up. What follows is a meditation you can use to ask your guides for information in waking dreams. Try doing this exercise before going to bed to create a dreamtime connection with your spirit guides.

- Think about a question that you would like to have some insight into and write it in a dream journal or on a notepad.
- Ask your guides to connect to you and set the intention that you wish to meet your guides that night in your dreams. Read the question aloud before going to bed, and leave your written question next to your bed.

- Remain open to the idea that your guide could present itself as an animal or a person. It may also just come as a feeling you have throughout the dream, and when you wake, you just intuitively know what to do.
- Write down what you can remember upon waking so you can reflect on it during the day.

My own experiences with my spirit guides in dreams can vary. But the ones that stick with me the most are the ones where they come with messages or a feeling of reassurance and guidance. I always wake with a good feeling that there is some message there, and sometimes I just need to reflect on it to find out what it is.

Lucid Dreaming

Lucid dreaming, which aligns more closely to the mainstream Western view of dreaming, is used in shamanic cultures to receive information and messages. It is a skill that requires a lot of practice. Shamans or dream walkers are often called upon to have a dream that shows them the right way to heal a patient, and before going to sleep they will ask for insight into the issue. Sometimes the shaman meets guides in a dream that help them find a lost soul or enable them to shape-shift a negative force and get rid of it.

Some of you may be aware that you astral project during your sleep. This is different from lucid dreaming, because during astral projection you are called by a spirit or higher beings to help others in another dimension. If you are already working in a spiritual manner as a "light worker," your services may be required to come to the aid of another person's soul.

9

A SPIRIT QUEST

Going on a quest is a powerful way to connect yourself to the earth and nature and open up spiritually. You can take a journey into nature for solitude and introspection and to find the answers to personal questions.

The traditional way of doing this is by sitting outside and asking for a vision to give guidance about something the person needed to know or about their role in life. The length of the vision quest varies, but in some traditions, questers stay for around four days and nights, usually without food, and in some traditions, without water. This is absolutely *not* something that you should attempt.

In some cultures, the spirit quest is a rite of passage into adulthood, with the visions a young person receives helping to determine the roles they will play as members of their community. They continue to use the ritual during adulthood whenever they need help from the spirit realm and animal or power guides.

This kind of vision quest is a religious experience based on the earth, the sky, and other elements of nature. We are surrounded with messages and signs from the spiritual realms, and the vision quest allows us to be still and to go within so that we can hear these messages.

In some shamanic traditions, someone wanting to go on a vision quest climbs a mountain or goes to a special place—perhaps a sacred site or perhaps a "dreaming place" (usually a pit dug out of the side of a hill). Sometimes the person sits at the center of a circle of stones, known as a medicine wheel, created by the tribe as a safe and holy place and used for generations. (For more on the medicine wheel, see chapter 13.)

If you are setting out to develop spiritually, a vision quest can help, and there are many ways to embark upon your own version. It can be as simple as sitting in the woods or walking in nature while looking at the plants and other surroundings.

Undertaking a vision quest can help you to discover who you are, to define your goals in life, to find your purpose, and to gain power and clarity. It can help you to connect to your higher self and to nature. You can meet your guides, totems, and helpers. For some people, a vision quest can help them to overcome fears, heal abuse, cope with grief, handle anger issues, and resolve any past or current relationship issues.

The Shamanic Walk of Intention

A walk of intention is a way for a shaman to be "in their power," which means being able to use, control, and direct their spiritual abilities. They can do this by experiencing a shift in energy and using it to relate to nature and the world around them. Taking conscious walks like this is an easy and pleasant way to enhance your awareness of yourself and nature. During these walks you can connect to spirits and be in contact with your guides. All you need to do is

listen and be aware—don't hurry these walks. Meander slowly, with intention, your mind fixed on the purpose of the walk.

I usually start my walks of intention by getting anything off my chest that is bothering me. I do this by speaking out loud to my guides; it's like talking things through with an old friend who's always there for you and always ready to listen. Sometimes I ask for advice and guidance on how best to deal with a situation or person. Once I have shaken off this pent-up energy, I feel more relaxed, my mind is clearer, and I'm more open to receiving messages. I ask my guides and spirit helpers to show me what I need to know in order to proceed on my spiritual journey. I ask them to show me the way and to put signs in my path in a way that I'm able to understand.

On the other hand, sometimes I just walk without deliberately thinking of anything and instead just focus on being content to take in the nature around me. Even so, useful thoughts and ideas come into my mind. By the time I'm ready to go home, I have usually solved the answers to questions I didn't even know I had, found a renewed focus, and become energized. If you don't already walk with intention, I would highly recommend you give it a try and do it at least once a week.

10

SOUL RETRIEVAL

Shamans believe that part of the human soul is free to leave the body. It will do this when a person dreaming, or to protect itself from damaging emotional or physical situations. If the soul doesn't come back of its own accord, a shaman can intervene and return the soul to a person.

Tip

Shamans themselves can change their state of consciousness, allowing their free souls to travel and to retrieve ancient wisdom or to regain lost power.

Soul Loss

There are various reasons for soul loss, all of which are normal ways of the soul protecting itself. Here are some examples:

- A soul may leave to protect itself when the person is in an abusive situation.
- Frightened children may send their souls to hide while their parents are fighting.
- The soul may jump out of the body just before an accident in order to avoid the force of the accident.
- If someone is grieving a death, the bereaved person's soul may leave until the person is ready to deal with their grief.

In some cases, the missing part of the soul will return on its own, but in other cases, it may not know how to return or may not know that it's safe to do so. When this happens, a shaman may need to assist in returning the missing piece.

Another way to lose one's soul is to give it to someone else. This happens sometimes when two people are in love or when they are in a very loving family —a mother may give some of her soul to her child because she wishes to protect the child, or a lover may give a part of their soul to the other so they can remain close to them all the time.

Frankly, this is not a good idea. Nobody can actually use another person's soul, and all that happens is that the loved one has to cope with this extra energy in addition to dealing with their own problems. Also, the person who gave their soul loses power, which may make them feel disconnected and upset. So, in the end, both people lose something.

Of course, most of the time, people don't know they are soul sharing, because in mainstream culture we never learn about it. However, there is a kind of inward "knowing" that we still have. For instance, you might hear of someone who "lost themselves" when they broke up with a partner, or you may hear someone saying their ex "stole their life."

Soul stealing is another reason for soul loss, and again, the subject doesn't usually realize they have taken someone else's soul. This is different from someone giving you their soul out of love, though soul stealing can be done quite innocently and accidentally. For example, you may know someone who is always happy, with lots of positive energy, and you want some of it. Or you may be afraid of losing someone, so you inadvertently take a piece of that person with you so that you will always have them close by.

In a way, this explains the difficulty some people have in letting go of past relationships, which can be not only an emotional attachment but a real physical attachment because they are unwittingly carting around a segment of the other person's soul. Under those circumstances, it is easy to understand why the person is so reluctant to let the person and the past go. The same goes for those who have given part of their own soul to someone who subsequently splits from them, because they are missing a bit of themselves. These situations need spiritual help, and that is where a shaman can be so very useful.

Soul stealing can be a way of dominating someone else, because when one person takes another's soul, he or she takes control of that person's power. This is, of course, exactly why a bullying abuser does it, even if they don't know or understand exactly what it is they are doing. If someone has stolen a piece of your soul, or if you have given it away or allowed someone to help themselves to it, you need to get it back.

You may also be able to stop soul loss before it happens if you become aware that someone is tugging at your soul. Once you recognize this, tell yourself firmly that they cannot have your soul. If you don't allow it, and you are absolutely clear in your own mind that they can't have it, they will find that they can't take it from you. This kind of thing deprives bullies of their power.

The following symptoms may indicate soul loss to a shaman:

- Depression.
- Feeling incomplete
- Inability to move forward on some issue
- Feeling like you're no longer in control of your life
- A patient saying, "I felt like part of me died when . . ."
- A patient saying, "I feel like this person has stolen my soul . . ."
- Memories or an incident in a patient's past that causes them to say, "I feel like I lost something that I never got back . . ."
- A sense by the patient that someone has taken a part of them—their heart or soul—or that they have not been the same since the person left or died
- A desire to return to an unhealthy relationship
- A desire to return to a specific place when there is no good reason to do so

Being in a coma is a situation of extreme soul loss—when someone is in a coma, more of the soul is out of the body than is in it. If the body is in a great deal of pain, or if the soul needs time to heal and to consider its situation, a coma provides the time needed. Shock is another symptom of soul loss.

Retrieving the Soul

The reality is that we can't do this for ourselves, so we need to seek out a shaman to do this for us, but if you are unable to do this, there are ways in which you can help make your situation better. You can put the question to the universe before meditating or journeying, you can ask for a healing dream, or you can ask your guardian spirit or power animal to return your soul to you in pieces.

Shamans who suspect soul loss will generally perform a shamanic journey to find out whether the patient does indeed need a part of their soul returned. Then they will take a journey to retrieve the soul pieces and blow each piece back into the body of the patient, one at time, focusing until the soul's essence fills that person's body.

When performing soul retrieval, the shaman will create a sacred space for the patient that protects them from interference from the outside world. The experience is perfectly safe.

People's reactions after soul retrieval can be varied—after all, each one of us is unique and so is the returning soul. If you embark on this, it's important not to have any preconceived ideas about what you might feel. Some people feel great joy, some feel sadness, some feel lighter or heavier, and some people feel nothing at all. That said, some of the benefits experienced by people who have received soul retrieval include finding it easier to make decisions; having a sense of being more present in their life; being able to move forward regarding an issue that they couldn't cope with before; being able to begin dealing with loss and grief; and having the hope or the confidence to find someone new or to start something new in their life. In general, people tend to feel able to start the healing process that they so desperately need.

The most important thing is to be open-minded when considering shamanic sessions. Understand that this will help you to receive your lost soul part back and allow you to see past the problem and to spot new things that you need to bring into your life. Maybe you need to have more fun or you need to go out more. Perhaps you need to give yourself some quiet time to go within yourself. You must listen to yourself if you are to allow changes to happen in your life, and you need to take care of yourself even if it means putting your needs above others' so you can start to feel like yourself again.

The Soul Catcher

A soul catcher is an amulet used by shamans of the Pacific Northwest Coast. It looks like a tube slightly flaring at the ends and in some cultures is carved of mountain goat bone or out of wood, with carvings that represent the shaman's tribe and spirit helpers. It is also decorated with small shell pieces and bone that represent teeth that highlight the animals, which are often wolves and sea lions. Some are fitted with a bark stopper at each end. A shaman wears the soul catcher around their neck when performing soul retrieval ceremonies.

Finding the Right Healer

If you need a shamanic healer, you should look for someone who practices shamanic rituals or healing fairly regularly and has the right experience. It is always best to go by a recommendation by someone you know and trust or to ask to speak to someone whom the shaman has worked with. However, the most important thing is how you feel about the shaman personally: work out for yourself whether you feel comfortable in their presence and feel as though you would be in capable hands.

Some people feel that they need support after healing or soul retrieval, and in this case, your shamanic practitioner may be able to help you. I know that after I have done any form of healing, I check on the person a few days later to see how they are. If a shamanic practitioner cares enough to help people, they should care enough to see how the person feels afterward.

Indeed, the real benefit of soul retrieval or any shamanic healing is the knowledge that someone cares enough to listen and help. Most shamanic practitioners and healers feel a strong desire to help make people's lives a little easier, and some patients say that this is one of the most helpful parts of the healing process. It is good for both shaman and patient to build a lasting working relationship.

❉ ❉ ❉

11

CEREMONIES
AND RITUALS

Shamanic ceremonies work better in groups due to the amount of energy that is created by multiple people, but you can also practice some alone. You can use ceremonies to connect with spirits, to mark times of transition, to connect with nature, to make things happen, to achieve healing, or to release and let go of something. You just have to choose your intention. Once you have given some thought to the purpose of your ceremony, you will need to create your sacred space, and this can be done either outdoors or inside.

You will need the following tools:

- A compass
- A sage bunch
- A bell, drum, or rattle (see pages 26 and 30 for more on these tools)
- Flowers, stones, candles, crystals, or other favorite objects

Creating Sacred Space for an Outdoor Shamanic Ceremony

- Make a circle with stones and mark out the north, south, east, and west.
- Sweep the area and clean it by walking round with a lit bunch of sage—a practice called smudging. You can also use sound, such as your bell, drum, or rattle.
- Create an altar using flowers, stones, candles, crystals—any objects really that you feel would be appropriate to the ceremony.
- Call in spirits, guides, or higher beings and ask for protection, blessings, and guidance while you perform your ceremony.
- Walk around the inside of your stone circle or sit inside it, as you wish. You can chant, sing, or meditate, or you could hit your drum or shake your rattle. In short, just go with the flow.
- When you have finished, clear everything away and thank your spirits or helpers.

Creating Sacred Space for an Indoor Shamanic Ceremony

- Make sure the room you have chosen has been tidied, cleaned, and refreshed.
- Place a cloth over a table or sideboard and set up your altar items.
- Smudge the area with burning sage or burn incense. Call in your spirit guides for protection and blessings while you stand or sit in front of your altar to perform your ritual.
- You can write a note of the things you want to say or to achieve, and you can sing and chant or dance if you wish. Do whatever feels right for you at the time.
- When you have finished, you can clear everything away if you want to or leave it out to use again next time. Remember to thank your spirits.

Performing Seasonal Ceremonies

Shamans use the cycles of the moon and other elements of nature to perform ceremonies. Shamans mark the beginning and end of the seasons, honoring the equinoxes and solstices and connecting to the natural rhythms of nature. This importance of the cycles is also observed among other cultures and traditions, as we can see from sacred sites such as Stonehenge, which is built in alignment with the position of the sun on the solstices.

Spiritual energy is especially strong at these times, so ceremonies can produce amazing results. Equinoxes and solstices are great for healing, manifesting new conditions, or letting go of old and outdated ideas and problems. They clear space to allow room for new ideas, dreams, and projects to enter your life. These rituals can help you all throughout the year.

On the spring equinox, which occurs around March 21 in the Northern Hemisphere, the length of the day and the length of the night are the same. Spring is about sowing real and metaphorical seeds, planting new intentions, and releasing blocks that stop us from moving forward.

The summer solstice in the Northern Hemisphere is around June 21, and it is the longest day and shortest night of the year. It is also the first day of summer. Everything is in bloom, the sun is shining, and many wedding ceremonies are performed during this time of year.

The autumn equinox occurs around September 21 in the Northern Hemisphere. As on the spring equinox, the day and night are of equal length, but now the days will become shorter and the darkness will grow. This is the time of harvest and of being quiet, gathering knowledge, and planning for new ventures.

Tip

When it is the summer solstice in the Northern Hemisphere, it is the winter solstice in the Southern Hemisphere. Similarly, the spring equinox in the Northern Hemisphere is the fall equinox in the Southern Hemisphere.

The winter solstice in the Northern Hemisphere occurs around December 21, and it is the time of the year when the night is the longest and the day is the shortest. This is the best time to set up new ideas and to release old grudges and negative feelings.

Ritual Trance Dance

Shamanic ritual trance dances are held in a sacred space and accompanied by drumming. This ancient technique is used to shift the shaman's state of consciousness to enable them to enter the world of spirit and discover wisdom, guidance, healing, and visions. This inner journey is often done at night to allow the shaman to focus and see the visions.

Indigenous cultures all over the world use a dance of this kind, and many believe the spirits of animals and nature can empower them with courage and reveal insights into the future. These rituals may be used to help those suffering from spirit illness, which may manifest as depression or anxiety. It is also sometimes practiced as an initiation process for the younger members of a tribe.

There are many places in the world you can travel to and take part in a ritual trance dance. You may be blindfolded, and there will almost certainly be powerful and hypnotic music, designed to make you go deep within. There may be sounds from nature along with the beating of a drum. You can perform a solo dance, but you will not be alone, as there will be a group of people around you. You may feel uncomfortable to start with, but once you get into it, you will start to feel good—and after the dance, you will feel amazing. You can find ritual music online and practice dancing by yourself. As long as you have room to do this without bumping into furniture, you will be perfectly safe.

If you are going to practice dancing at home, here are some techniques that may help:

- As you start to feel the music, begin swaying, then progress into making flowing movements with your body.
- When you are comfortable with this, make short, sharp moves while you become more aware of your space and the rhythm and start to feel more at one with it.
- Allow your moves to become more chaotic as you let go and surrender yourself. Dance without inhibition.

- When you feel stillness within you, this shows that you have become the essence of the dance, as you move with the beat and become one with the music.

Moon Rituals

Each month, we have a new moon and a full moon (sometimes more than one). This means there are at least two opportunities each month to use the energy of the moon to help you bring new things into your life and to release and get rid of anything that you feel is not working or serving a purpose in your life. These rituals are best done outside in view of the moon, although you can't always do this during bad weather.

The time of the new moon is good for creating new beginnings, manifesting, setting intentions, and dreaming up new ideas and projects.

The time of the full moon helps with releasing anything that's no longer serving you, such as bad relationships, addictions, negative patterns, pain, fear, or obstacles.

For both of these ritual types, it is best to write down what you want to achieve and then light a candle and spend time thinking or meditating on what you want. Send your intentions out to the universe. Then, burn the piece of paper with your writing on it and toss out the ashes onto the earth when you have finished with them.

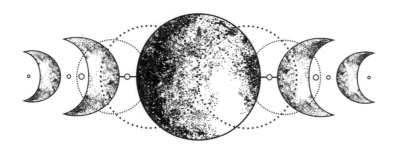

Sweat Lodges

A practice among some Native American tribes, a sweat lodge is a temporary domed structure created for the purpose of a ceremony or ritual. The sweat lodge ceremony or purification ritual is timed with important events, such as a rite of passage ceremony or a marriage. It may also be part of a healing ritual. A sweat lodge may also be called a medicine lodge or medicine house.

Traditionally, it was only a shaman who would build a sweat lodge, although he would employ members of the tribe to work on erecting sweat lodges under his instruction. Today, shamans will often help build them. Stones can be heated in a fire outside the lodge, brought inside, and placed in a pit under the center of the dome, where cold water is poured on them to create the steam that will purify and cleanse the participants in the ritual.

The ideal location for a sweat lodge is near water. The entrance, which is generally a small doorway one must crawl through, faces the west. The frame of the lodge is built of wood—specifically saplings, of the kind you would find on a willow tree. Poles are placed in the earth and then bent over to form the dome structure, then tied in place with twine. Animal skins are traditionally used to cover the framework and keep in the heat, and a movable flap covers the entrance. A small, shallow pit is dug in the center of the dome for the hot stones, and the floor is covered with aromatic herbs and sage. The shaman places a symbol of their spirit guide or power animal at the entrance—for example, the skull of an animal. The participants then crawl through the opening and sit in darkness in a circle. The sweat lodge is usually just big enough for a few people, although it may hold ten or more.

Under the leadership of the shaman, participants generally follow a ritual in four parts. They smoke a pipe of tobacco, which is filled and lit four times. The ceremony begins when the shaman conducts an opening prayer with the pipe raised to the mother sky, the father earth, and the four directions. The pipe then is passed around the circle and smoked by each person in turn, and the participants shake their rattles and sing sacred songs and incantations as the shaman summons the power of their animal guide. At the end of the first part of the ritual, the rattles are shaken four times, and then a second set of heated rocks is placed in the center to mark the beginning of the second stage. Prayers are offered to the universe, plants, animals, water, and spirits while the pipe is passed around again. The participants chant and shake rattles again.

Warning There are many ceremonies and rituals from around the world that include smoking a pipe, but I *do not* recommend smoking anything.

The third stage includes prayers for all the participants and their families, and the ritual is again repeated. The fourth stage includes prayers for strength and to the spirit deities, and the ritual is repeated again. In some cases, for several hours before the ceremony, participants prepare themselves by fasting.

These ceremonies typically last three to four hours, broken into rounds of twenty to thirty minutes, but this will vary from lodge to lodge. Participants are often only permitted to leave the lodge when the ceremony is finished. Practices have evolved over time, and not all ceremonies use a pipe these days.

The sweat lodge offers both physical cleansing, through the heat and steam and the medicinal herbs that are strewn around, and a mental and spiritual cleanse, enabling those present to go within themselves and gain clarity to see who they really are. It is a sacred way to find a true path in life and let go of limiting beliefs, behaviors, and patterns.

12

SHAMANIC DIVINATION

Shamans around the world use different tools and techniques to help them divine what is ailing a person physically or spiritually as well as answer questions and see what may be coming in the future.

Oracle Cards

Different oracle cards can use different art and symbolism. I have a deck of shaman oracle cards inspired by cave art that was created by our distant ancestors. No one really knows what those ancient paintings meant or what purpose they served, but the images on them still seem to resonate with us today and they are fascinating to see. These cards  help me tap into the primal wisdom that our ancestors had. Today's world may be very different, but we still have the same need for security, love, and meaning in our lives.

We can use shamanic techniques to journey into the different realms of spirit to find answers to our questions. Oracle cards help us do this through meditation and the symbolic images. If you decide to use cards, you will need to take some time to connect with your deck and become familiar with the images. There are a variety of oracle cards on the market, and a look online will show you what is available. Choose those to which you feel drawn.

Throwing the Bones

Shamans use natural objects in much the same way as tarot cards or runes. These objects can include the bones from chickens, rats, and other small animals along with shells, large seeds, colored stones, feathers, or anything else that helps the shaman to see, hear, and feel.

Dowsing

Part of the sangoma traditions of southern Africa is learning to dowse. Sangomas don't use rods or pendulums, as in some practices from other cultures, but instead feel the atmosphere with their hands, minds, and auras. This isn't particularly difficult for a sensitive person to do, especially if they work in the psychic sphere.

Candles

Candles have been used in divination for thousands of years in many cultures around the world. This method of candle reading has been in use in some South American cultures since ancient times and is still practiced today.

The shaman gives the patient a candle, which they rub over their fully clothed body, including the face and hands; then the shaman takes the candle and lights it. If the candle goes out right away, that indicates the person's health or even their life expectancy is not good, so healing will definitely be recommended. The shaman will then give the patient a fresh candle and tell them to start again. If the candle stays lit right from the start, the shaman moves on to interpret the flame. Although the art of candle reading is complex, an introduction to some of the basic insights a shaman may glean based on colors seen in the flame follows here.

Blue

The patient copes well with life and may also be clairvoyant. Dark blue at the bottom of the flame suggests poor digestion and childhood traumas that are still being carried around—often something to do with the relationship to the mother.

Purple

The person is quick to anger and finds it hard to control their temper.

Tip

Palmists also know about purple fingers, which may indicate a choleric nature, raised cholesterol, and blocked heart arteries.

Red

This patient is suffering from anger that may at times be turned inward, leading to health problems.

Yellow

This patient has a happy and generous nature and should have a good life. They are a good student or teacher.

Orange

The patient has a positive nature and good health. They should make a success of whatever they are doing at the time of the reading.

Green

There are two possibilities here. Pale green shows that the patient is good at making money, while darker green indicates feelings of jealousy and spite.

Black, Gray, Brown

Unsurprisingly, these colors suggest sickness, depression, fear, or trauma from which the patient has not recovered. Healing would be recommended here.

The Wick and the Flame

The wick represents the body of the patient, so the shaman will study it to see which part might be out of shape, as it could indicate a mental or physical problem. A high flame shows a spiritual nature, while a low, fat flame shows a need for financial and emotional security.

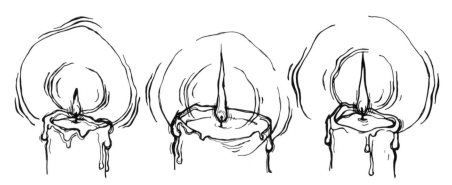

Scrying the Flame

Scrying through fire is surprisingly easy to do for someone who has trained in the divination arts. The shaman lights a candle and sits back from it, then starts to gaze into the flame while allowing themselves to slip into a slightly trancelike state. As their eyes glaze over, they begin to see visions in the flames that sharpen into clear pictures in their mind's eye. If both the shaman and the patient are clairvoyant, they may pick up the same visions at the same time!

Sand Reading and Geomancy

Sand reading comes from Egypt. The shaman has a deep tray that contains sand, sometimes mixed with small pebbles, which they have charged with prayers and light and blessed for their patients. The patient is asked to stir or mix the sand around for a few minutes, and then the shaman reads the sand in much the same way that one reads tea leaves in a cup. One part of the tray relates to events within the home and family, one indicates events outside or related to the career, one denotes the patient themselves, one concerns those who are around them, one shows happiness and another sadness, and so on.

Geomancy is reading the land. In one geomancy practice from West African countries, including Nigeria and Ghana, the shaman chooses a small patch of ground and marks it out with pegs of wood. They then tie a length of string to the peg at the corner of the piece of ground and wind the string around the wood, creating a diamond-shaped area. Each diamond area has a meaning— the shaman might lay out one for the patient, one for their parents, one for their partner, one for their children, one for their work, one for their health, and many other such divisions. He leaves the pattern overnight. The next morning, the shaman examines the ground for animal prints and interprets their meaning according to the size and type of animal that left the print and the precise diamond area the animal trod on.

13

THE MEDICINE WHEEL

A medicine wheel can be used as a tool for enlightenment and guidance in much the way that astrology is used. For instance, a practitioner can advise a questioner on the direction to travel in order to improve his or her life. Someone who has studied the medicine wheel system in depth can give worthwhile advice on health, career matters, neighborhood problems, relationships, and finances, in much the same way as an astrologer does.

The word *medicine* in this context means something like "putting things in order and creating harmony" so it has nothing to do with doctors or conventional medicine as we know it. It can relate to healing and mending in the sense of helping individual people, but it can also refer to improving the condition of the environment and the need for balance and harmony within the earth, sky, rivers and lakes, animals, plants, and humans.

The medicine wheel is a mix of old and modern ideas. Indeed, the name itself is relatively modern, while the rock formations—natural and otherwise—that form the background to this idea are ancient. There are many possible origins, but the round design of the medicine wheel may have originated among the Mayan or Aztec wheel calendars. Some farming calendars used in the southern parts of the United States are likewise rooted in Aztec or Mayan wheel calendars.

Western New Age thinking uses the medicine wheel as a tool for personal development, but Native Americans use it as a ceremonial design, and throughout the United States you can find

A stone medicine wheel

examples of medicine wheels marked out on the ground with stones that have stood for centuries. These are linked to the movement of the sun and moon, and they may function like miniature versions of the kind of ancient stone circles that we see in Stonehenge or Avebury in England.

Astrology, Seasons, and Directions

Before we get to the medicine wheel system, we need to look at our familiar astrology, because that will make it easier to understand the medicine wheel system.

Before people understood how the solar system worked, sky watchers the world over thought the sun orbited the earth rather than the other way around, but they also realized that the sun's position had something to do with the seasons and the compass points. In Western astrology, the cardinal signs of Aries, Cancer, Libra, and Capricorn mark the start of each season, and these signs also link with the cardinal points of the compass, as shown here. It may seem odd that the summer solstice links with the cold north, and the winter one with the hot south—at least in the Northern Hemisphere—but there are complex astrological and geographic reasons for this.

As you will see, Western astrology and the medicine wheel are remarkably similar in their approach. Here are the two systems, each showing the seasons and directions.

Sign	Season	Direction
Aries	Spring equinox	East
Cancer	Summer solstice	North
Libra	Autumn equinox	West
Capricorn	Winter solstice	South

Power Animal	Season	Direction
Buffalo	Winter	North
Golden Eagle	Spring	East
Coyote	Summer	South
Grizzly Bear	Autumn	West

Times of the Day

A Western astrology chart links with the times of the day, showing dawn on the left-hand side of the chart, noon at the top, sunset on the right, and midnight at the bottom of the chart. The medicine wheel, too, marks the turning points of each day, and each of the power animals is associated with a particular time:

- The White Buffalo sits at the top of the wheel, ruling the period after midnight.

- The Golden Eagle is located on the right side of the wheel and connects with the sunrise and early morning.

- The Coyote is found at the bottom of the wheel and is associated with noon.

- The Grizzly Bear sits on the left of the wheel, where he presides over sunset.

Stages of Life and Activities

The medicine wheel also represents the stages of life: childhood, young adulthood, maturity, and old age. The astrological power animals are linked to certain activities, such as hunting, lovemaking, and so on.

The Native American Clans

The Medicine Wheel is linked to Native American astrology, which seems to have evolved out of older systems that are linked to the Aztec farming calendar and to weather and seasonal changes. There are four clans, which are the Turtle, the Butterfly, the Frog, and the Thunderbird, although some tribes prefer to use the Falcon rather than the mythical Thunderbird. Their main use is much the same as that of the elements in Western astrology, as each has a nature of its own. For instance, a Snow Goose belongs to the Turtle clan, and the energies of this clan are similar to the earth energies in Western astrology. This links well, because the sign for this time of the year in Western astrology is Capricorn, which is an earth sign.

Each of the Native American signs of the zodiac is linked to one of four clans as follows:

Zodiac Sign	Clan
Snow Goose	Turtle
Otter	Butterfly
Cougar	Frog
Red Hawk	Thunderbird/Falcon
Beaver	Turtle
Deer	Butterfly
Flicker	Frog
Sturgeon	Thunderbird/Falcon
Brown Bear	Turtle
Raven	Butterfly
Snake	Frog
Elk	Thunderbird/Falcon

The Power Animals

Native American astrology uses the four power animals to depict the turning points of each season. Some tribes use different animals besides the Buffalo, Golden Eagle, Coyote, and Grizzly Bear, and some of these alternatives are listed on the following pages. Each animal connects to a variety of corresponding ideas. The way to use them is partly as a timing device, so you know when to make changes or start something new, and partly as advice on what direction to take for good fortune or to find love, financial gain, or whatever is needed.

THE TURTLE CLAN

The Turtle is associated with the earth element. It is considered slow, persevering, determined, and capable. The clan image is one of solid reliability, doing a job well and finishing what one starts.

THE BUTTERFLY CLAN

Associated with the air element, the Butterfly represents transformation due to its ability to grow out of a caterpillar. This clan rules the idea of communication, because the Butterfly moves swiftly from one place to another. It relates to movement, ideas, change, and renewal.

THE FROG CLAN

This clan is related to the element of water, and it is linked to intuition and the ability to pick up on the energies around it. Frogs and toads live in water but also on land, so they can adapt to a variety of situations. They represent creativity, flexibility, and the ability to listen to others and perhaps also to counsel them.

THE THUNDERBIRD OR FALCON CLAN

Associated with the element of fire, this clan represents the start of something, the inspiration that gets something off the ground, along with enthusiasm, liveliness, courage, and a sense of fun.

An illustration of a medicine wheel

THE WHITE BUFFALO

Main Power Animal	White Buffalo
Alternative Power Animals	Moose, Bear
Direction	North
Season	Winter
Time	After midnight
Weather	Very cold
Age Group	Old age
Activity	Rest, repairs, recovery, lovemaking
Mineral	Alabaster
Element	Earth
Plant	Sweetgrass

The White Buffalo, the Bear, and the Moose all rule the north, the winter, and the nighttime. They denote a time to rest, sleep, and dream.

These animals cope well with the cold or hibernate during the depths of winter. They grow layers of fat to see them through the season; they move slowly, sleep a lot, and forage when times are good. The winter is a quiet time when things appear to be dormant—nothing is growing, and time stands still.

This is the time of the year in which to rest and take things easy. It is a time for peace, forgiveness, and compassion. It is a time for hunting and fishing, because the people still need to eat and to have protein to give them strength. Fish and meat can be salted and preserved to see them through the lean times.

This period is also associated with older people, who are at the stage in their lives when they are slowing down.

The element that rules is that of earth, which represents slow movement, steadfastness, reliability, and obstinacy. While the earth is usually unchanging, it can move with great force, such as in an earthquake or a volcanic eruption.

The White Buffalo is associated with intuition, dreams, and clairvoyance, and during this quiet time of the year, people may be more intuitive than usual.

THE GOLDEN EAGLE

Main Power Animal	Golden Eagle
Alternative Power Animals	Hummingbird, Owl, Hawk
Direction	East
Season	Spring
Time	Sunrise and early morning
Weather	Changeable
Age Group	Youth
Activity	Planting, young animals, fresh starts
Mineral	Catlinite
Element	Air
Plant	Tobacco

The Golden Eagle, Hummingbird, Owl, and Hawk are all birds, suggesting a need for freedom and the ability to see things from a distance.

As far as timing is concerned, these power animals represent the rising sun and the early morning as well as the springtime. As in most divinatory systems, springtime represents birth, youth, beginnings, and a cheerful and optimistic frame of mind. Those who are born at this time of year are good at starting new things, coming up with new ideas, and finding opportunities for progress. They can use their knowledge of the spiritual realms to help those on the earth.

Unsurprisingly, these bird totems are associated with the element of air, which enhances the idea of being able to go anywhere at a moment's notice. Air is also associated with communication, and this sign is interested in writing, broadcasting, teaching, and working in a communicative field. The age group associated with the Golden Eagle is youth.

THE COYOTE

Main Power Animal	Coyote
Alternative Power Animals	Lion, Wolf
Direction	South
Season	Summer
Time	Noon
Weather	Very hot
Age Group	Young adulthood
Activity	Sex, passion, birth, hunting, fighting
Mineral	Serpentine
Element	Fire
Plant	Sage bush

The Coyote, Lion, and Wolf are predators who usually hunt in packs, although they are all capable of hunting alone. They are connected with summer, a time

of abundance. This time links to the energy demanded by sex and passion, and the outcome of the lovemaking is traditionally childbirth, so this is a good time to start a family. The time linked with the Coyote is midday, the busiest time of the day when much can be accomplished.

The fire element suggests pride, achievement, and passionate love, which fits with the vigor and confidence of adulthood. The image is that of strength, agility, ability, and success at the hunt or in family and tribal life.

Those born during this phase are confident and energetic, so they tend to be successful. They continue to learn throughout life and don't give up easily, but they can also be dishonest and unreliable.

THE GRIZZLY BEAR

Main Power Animal	Grizzly Bear
Alternative Power Animals	Beaver, Snake
Direction	West
Season	Autumn
Time	Sunset
Weather	Cooling down, changeability
Age Group	Maturity, middle age
Activity	Harvest
Mineral	Soapstone
Element	Water
Plant	Cedar tree

The Grizzly Bear is extremely powerful, the Beaver is very industrious, and the Snake just gets on with its life, finding enough to eat and keeping out of trouble as far as it can. All three of these animals can be sleepy during the winter, so they have to stock up their reserves during the abundant time of the autumn. The time ruled by the Grizzly Bear is the sunset, when things are cooling down and animals are starting to settle down for the night.

People come together to gather in the harvest, to preserve meat, and to can fruits and vegetables. Autumn is the time to give thanks for the harvest and the results of hunting trips and pray for the health and strength to get through the coming winter. Once the harvest is safely in and the food, skins, and other implements have been cleaned and put away, the tribe can start to relax. It is a time of assessment and reassessment, when people can look at what they have achieved during the previous year and make plans for the coming year.

The water element is somewhat feminine and rather like yin in Chinese astrology in that it rules love, trust, compassion, sensuality, fertility, and resilience. The age group is middle age, a time of continued vigor and activity but also of wisdom and the accumulation of knowledge. This symbolizes the end of one road and clearing the way in preparation for the start of a new phase.

14

NATIVE AMERICAN SOLAR ASTROLOGY

It is not easy to discover which Native American tribes used astrology, but we know that people took a renewed interest in it during the New Age boom of the 1970s. We also know that this is when the dates of the astrological animal signs were aligned to the zodiac signs in Western astrology. Now the system is known and understood around the world. For example, the Snow Goose fits the time frame for Capricorn in Western astrology, but it can also suggest that the dates will be significant in the person's future. The individual may need to take advice from the earth-element of the Turtle and focus on small details rather than try to deal with everything at once. A birch tree can cope with winter weather better than most, so this may denote a change in the subject's luck when winter comes. The person could consider using quartz for healing purposes or look out for something in white that will be significant to him or her.

The word *moon* in this system refers to months. The dates given in the Signs, Dates, Moons, and More chart on the following pages are the same every year. Astrologers know that from our perspective on Earth, the sun doesn't appear to move from one sign of the zodiac to another at exactly the same hour or even the same day ever year, but the Native American system is more general and doesn't take this into account.

Signs, Dates, Moons, and More

Animal Sign	Date	Moon
Snow Goose	Dec. 22–Jan. 19	Earth
Otter	Jan. 20–Feb. 18	Rest/Cleansing
Cougar	Feb. 19–March 20	Big Winds
Red-Tailed Hawk	March 21–April 19	Budding Trees
Beaver	April 20–May 20	Frogs Return
Deer	May 21–June 20	Corn Planting
Flicker	June 21–July 22	Strong Sun
Sturgeon	July 23–Aug. 22	Ripe Berries
Brown Bear	Aug. 23–Sept. 22	Harvest
Raven	Sept. 23–Oct. 23	Ducks Fly
Snake	Oct. 24–Nov. 21	Freeze Up
Elk	Nov. 22–Dec. 21	Long Snows

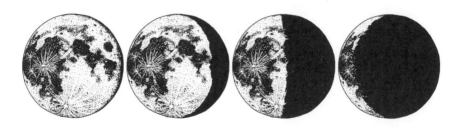

Plant	Mineral	Clan	Color
Birch Tree	Quartz	Turtle	White
Aspen	Silver	Butterfly	Silver
Plantain	Turquoise	Frog	Turquoise
Dandelion	Fire Opal	Thunderbird / Falcon	Yellow
Blue Camas	Chrysocolla	Turtle	Blue
Yarrow	Moss Agate	Butterfly	Pale Green
Wild Rose	Carnelian	Frog	Pink
Raspberry	Garnet	Thunderbird / Falcon	Red
Violet	Amethyst	Turtle	Purple
Mullein	Jasper	Butterfly	Brown
Thistle	Malachite	Frog	Orange
Spruce	Obsidian	Thunderbird / Falcon	Black

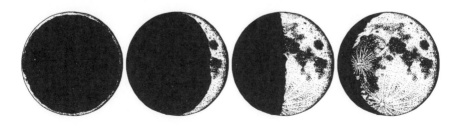

Animal Sign Variations

As in many forms of astrology, there are variations in names, so here are some commonly known alternatives:

ANIMAL SIGN	$\longrightarrow$	ALTERNATIVE
Cougar		Wolf
Red-Tailed Hawk		Falcon
Deer		Stag
Flicker		Woodpeckerr
Sturgeon		Salmon
Brown Bear		Bear
Elk		Owl

The Snow Goose

December 22–January 19

In its native habitat, the Snow Goose travels far and wide, so it knows how to conserve energy. In a person, this translates as someone who is cautious and careful with money. Snow Geese are shy, but when people get to know them, they show themselves to be sociable, kind, and helpful. The direction for this creature is north, which is where the Snow Goose lives.

This is an ambitious sign that is highly motivated and hardworking. Geese can climb the ladder of success by taking a sensible and planned approach to each step along the way. Their element is earth, which doesn't move very much and represents slow progress of the Goose as it flies through falling snow and high winds.

Snow Geese work hard—sometimes they take on too much and then have to cope with disappointment. These people sometimes need to step back, set easier goals, and worry less about their progress, and see the funny side of things. People born under this sign are devoted to their family and will never let their parents down. The Goose is a faithful lover who wants a quiet life; they don't enjoy arguments and instead want to be happy and make their loved ones happy. They may be most content in later life when they find the right person to love. They aren't overly keen on children and get on best with older people. This sign is linked to office jobs such as publisher, accountant, and lawyer as well as those with specialized knowledge, such as shipping and banking.

The Otter

January 20–February 18

This totem animal is linked to the north and the element of air, which suggests a love of communication. Like the playful creature that their sign is, Otter people have a reputation for being unconventional and unpredictable, and they are intelligent and inventive but a little impractical at times. They are excellent friends because of their honesty and desire to support others, and their generosity means they are great people to turn to in times of trouble.

Otters are known for being extremely curious, so they love reading and gathering data they can use to teach others. In conversation, they can get so excited and enthusiastic that they take over without realizing it, but they dislike it when others do the same thing to them. Many Otters prefer animals to people, and not all of them settle down into family life; some prefer not to have children. In general, however, this sign is quite friendly and agreeable.

Otters are original thinkers who can make careers out of computer technology, photography, and design. Many of them work in teaching; some love music and others are astrologers.

The Cougar

February 19–March 20

The Cougar (also known as the mountain lion, the puma, or sometimes even the panther) is mainly found in the western United States. It lives, as one of its names suggests, in mountainous areas, where it has learned to be a good climber. It can run quickly and roams far and wide. It is a predator that can hunt alone or in a family group. Its direction is the northeast, and its element is water. An alternative totem for this sign is the Wolf, which can also hunt alone or in a pack.

Cougars are adaptable and able to cope with a variety of circumstances, but they aren't powerful personalities. They are gentle and patient and can be impractical, indecisive, and easily led. They are kind, good-natured, and generous, and their sensitivity makes them compassionate and understanding. Cougars can be artistic or musical and can come up with really clever ideas; they are also intuitive and possibly clairvoyant, and they may use those skills in their work. Some Cougars can become too fond of food or alcohol. They can also be surprisingly spiteful and envious of others, though most Cougars are reasonable. Some Cougars end up bringing up grandchildren or looking after other family members.

The Cougar may work as a vet or nurse or in a charity. They may also choose to work as a ranger, looking after the countryside and the mountains where they can roam freely.

The Red-Tailed Hawk
March 21–April 19

The Red-Tailed Hawk is associated with the direction of east and the element of fire, which paints an image of someone who can find shelter and escape the cold easterly wind. Pueblo people refer to these birds as red eagles. They are said to have a special connection to the sky and the sun, which gives them magical powers, so this is a high-status bird. Its feathers are valued and often used in healing ceremonies. An alternative totem for this sign is the Falcon.

The Red-Tailed Hawk is decisive, capable, and efficient if sometimes unrealistic, and they can rise to the top of their career. They are also a good decision maker who can take on a challenge and has the courage to try new concepts. Their faults are selfishness, a high opinion of themselves, and a tendency to bully others. Some Red-Tailed Hawks don't relish family life, preferring the freedom to fly away at any time, but those who like being in a family value their partners and do their best for their children. They can be highly sexual, so they need a partner who is equally interested in lovemaking.

Ambitious and able, this totem can take a leading role in any job, and many go into politics, where their combination of true idealism and ability can take them to the top. The Red-Tailed Hawk is very good with young people, so they may also go into teaching.

The Beaver
April 20–May 20

This totem is linked to the direction of the east and to the element of the earth, despite the fact they spend their lives in rivers. Beavers are often considered anxious, but this tends to be because they like to keep moving—because being forced to stand still will annoy the industrious Beaver.

This sign is known for being determined, tenacious, and talented, so they do well with their work projects. They are also reliable when it comes to marriage and other long-term relationships, but they do tend to worry about money.

They need security for themselves and their families, and they also feel the need to live in their own houses, preferably with the mortgages paid off. They can be charitable when they have the means, but for the most part, their charity begins at home and with the family. The Beaver is a homebody, but they are also very sociable, so they love to entertain, and even when they travel they like to have their nearest and dearest with them. They can sometimes be too hardworking and need to learn to relax and to have fun. They seem calm on the outside, but they tend to worry and to become upset if they feel insecure.

The Beaver has a talent for making things, including for cooking or gardening. Many of this sign love to sing and dance, so they may join a choir or a dance team. Their love of earthy things makes many of them experts in everything to do with crystals.

The Deer

May 21–June 20

The Deer or Stag is connected to the earth and to the east. The earth connection gives them a great deal of common sense and the ability to work hard and finish the things they start—unless they become bored, that is. The east is the area connected to new ideas, novelties, and fresh starts, so if the Deer's life collapses around them, they can pick themselves up and start again.

Deer are kind-hearted people who love to help others, but they may not have a strong enough personality to take on those with really severe problems. They don't like arguments; they can stand up for themselves when necessary, but they find personal relationships quite difficult. This totem is very caring, but others can bore them to the point where they walk away, or they can become worn out by a demanding partner. They may find friendship easier than romantic relationships. Deer will try to bring people together and to create a sense of harmony and order in their world.

This sign is clever, amusing, and able to talk to everybody, so long as their nerves don't let them down. Indeed, they may be good teachers, broadcasters, journalists, entertainers, and public speakers. If they take up social work, they need to work in a team. They may be much better with animals than with people, and they could take in strays or other animals that need help.

The Flicker

June 21–July 22

The Flicker, a type of woodpecker, is a beautiful light-brown bird with black spots on its back and wings and a pretty red mark that looks like an upside-down stirrup on the back of its head. In some Native American traditions, the Flicker is connected to a goddess figure known as the Sacred Mother. The time of this sign is when the harvest starts, and there are a lot of young animals being born that can be hunted for meat later in the year.

This sign starts at the summer solstice and is connected to the direction of the south, which in the Northern Hemisphere represents heat and light. The element is water, which suggests that the Flicker is an emotional type who is sensitive to the atmosphere around them.

Flickers know intuitively when other people need help and are good at helping them, so this makes them good friends and pleasant companions. Many Flickers are more interested in love, romance, and relationships than work, and their interest in human relationships can make them successful novelists. However, these folks can be so keen to help and support their partners that they can lose their own identity and become absorbed by the other person. This is even more the case when Flickers have children, as they can become absorbed by their needs.

Flickers are good at business, especially the kind of business that serves the needs of the public, such as retail. They are clever with money, although they may not become rich because they refuse to sacrifice family life for financial gain.

Sturgeon

July 23–August 22

The Sturgeon, which many call the Salmon, is linked to the south-southwest and the element of fire. In the Northern Hemisphere, this represents the hottest time of the year and is during the harvest, so it is a time of plenty. It is said that Sturgeons can do anything they set their minds to, and it does seem to be the case, although they aren't keen on heavy-duty building work. These people are full of energy and enthusiasm and are goal oriented. Their powerful leadership qualities mean they not only can carry others with them but also have the tenacity to finish what they start.

Sturgeons are keen on family life, particularly their children, but if a family member hurts them, Sturgeons are quite capable of cutting them out of their lives. For the most part, these friendly people are very good company. They can have many partners, but once they make a commitment, they are loyal and faithful. They are good to those who need a helping hand and tend to fight for the underdog. They have a high opinion of themselves and can be arrogant.

This is a creative sign with a touch of glamour and show business about them, so they can be found in glamorous careers. However, they are also comfortable with technology and make excellent astrologers as well.

The Brown Bear

August 23–September 22

The Brown Bear, also simply called the Bear, is linked to the element of earth and the west-southwest. This is a large, powerful animal that has few, if any, predators. They love to hunt and to fish for their dinner. Female bears care for their young and teach them how to survive in their sometimes-difficult surroundings.

Humans born under the Brown Bear sign are practical and capable and love to learn, but they don't have a great deal of confidence, so they are often underestimated. They are a mixture of capable administrators and creative thinkers who can make beautiful things. Brown Bears have many friends, and they can attract downers at times, which is hard on them because they aren't terribly strong personalities themselves. If they decide on a particular career or way of life, they are very goal oriented and do well, and they never hurt or use others if they can help it.

This sign may not settle into marriage, but it is a sensual sign that needs a good sex life, so there may be a number of partners over the years. Brown Bears are extremely intuitive and have good judgment when it comes to others. They can be clairvoyant and particularly good at things like the tarot or the runes.

Some Brown Bears may be interested in writing, publishing, and broadcasting, but others are into building, decorating, and making furniture. They are young at heart and make wonderful friends.

The Raven

September 23–October 23

Unsurprisingly for a bird totem, the Raven is an air sign, which suggests a life with a certain amount of moving around. Its direction is west. These people can be extremely successful, especially in big business, because they set their minds on a target and aren't easily diverted from it. They need money, security, and a good way of life, and if they lose everything, they work hard to get back on their feet. Ravens can be good-looking, glamorous, and charismatic, and they are often the leaders of the pack. Almost everything they take on works out well for them in the end.

They like to look cool and aren't easily ruffled, but they can get angry at times. Ravens are intuitive and perceptive, so they see through those who seek to take them for fools, but they can use others if the prize is big enough. They are passionate lovers, and they may have many partners during their lifetime, sometimes more than one at a time, so while some Ravens enjoy family life, others may be too unsettled to stay in one relationship for long. They are artistic and intelligent and make wonderful friends.

Ravens love to travel and explore and may work in various interesting areas of the world, so they may not settle down until later in life. They make money in many forms of business, but they can spend it as fast as they make it.

The Snake

October 24–November 21

This sign is connected to the northwest and to the element of water. These correspondences make this sign cool on one hand but emotional on the other, so the Snake's feelings run deep. It is said that many shamans are born under this sign, so they become spiritual leaders and healers. They have an instinct for psychology and are quick to understand people while also being able to handle any problem that comes their way with a cool and calm approach.

Snakes often feel that others in their family are valued more highly than they are and grow up with a certain amount of resentment. Where love and marriage are concerned, they are either very loyal or totally unfaithful. They can be extremely generous to their loved ones or amazingly stingy. They may never drink alcohol or be absolute alcoholics. In short, they don't do anything by half.

Snakes are deep thinkers who know a great deal about their chosen subject. They are often drawn into the world of medicine and healing, but some make a life in the armed forces or the police, where their patriotism, courage, and ability to do their duty stand them in good stead. Some have a spiritual interest, but they don't always advertise this, so Snakes can be found in perfectly ordinary day jobs while also being witches or top-class spiritual mediums. They are good at keeping secrets. They relax by listening to music, and some play an instrument as a hobby.

The Elk or Owl

November 22–December 21

The Elk is associated with the northwest and the element of fire. Both the Elk and its alternative identity, the Owl, roam far and wide, but their natures are very different, so for our purposes, we will stick to the Elk totem.

Elks can do most things that they put their minds to and are especially good at building or any kind of engineering work. They are happy if their work takes them from place to place because they don't like to be tied down. They are optimistic, broad-minded, and very lucky, and they usually make friends quite easily. Elks can be silly at times, and some are positively accident prone, while others tend to inadvertently say embarrassing things. However, they are great fun and wonderful hosts, and they can cheer up everyone around them.

They are interested in spiritual matters, and their intuition is quite strong, so they may take up an interest in such things as the tarot or astrology. Too much pressure can get them down, and their nerves aren't that strong, so they need a partner or family to turn to when times are bad. Many Elks love their partners deeply, but some are too restless for married life. They get on well with young people and enjoy spending time with their children and grandchildren.

A job that seems to suit Elks very well is teaching, whether an academic subject or sports or both. Some are so humorous that they find careers in comedy.

❋ ❋ ❋

15

THE MANSIONS OF THE MOON

This is a highly technical area of shamanic astrology. It isn't one that Western astrologers often use, although it is known to skilled practitioners. This system is known in Vedic astrology, but it can also be seen in some stone circles, such as the one in Little Bighorn, Wyoming, that is divided into twenty-seven segments. This kind of stone circle may be something like a sundial or calendar of sorts.

There is very little written down about how this system was used beyond the ancient ideas that I have recorded on the following pages. The system shows what each day is useful for or what should be avoided on any specific day.

Going back in time, it is possible that each mansion was linked to a particular deity, and it seems likely that before certain important rituals were carried out, a shaman would offer a gift or sacrifice to the deity in question. Many of the descriptions reflect how little used this system is today. The roots of these beliefs are so old that they have gotten lost in the mists of time, and I only add this chapter to preserve such knowledge before everything about it is forever lost. Please look at the explanations of the mansions as interesting pieces of history, and take them on with a large pinch of salt.

The System

It takes just under twenty-eight days for the moon to complete its month, starting with the first day of the new moon. The mansion system starts at the spring equinox, which occurs when the sun is at 0° Aries. Each mansion measures 12°51' 26", which is the distance the moon moves during the course of a day.

If you want to try the system for yourself, check out an astrology app on your smartphone and find the exact degree of the sun and moon and check the list to see what the day will be good (or bad) for. The interpretations may appear strange, but they have come from the distant past and from European shamanic roots, where the ideas were different from ours.

The numbers listed with each mansion relate to its precise position. For example, the Second Mansion starts at 12°51' of Aries and goes through to 25°42' of Aries. The moon travels through one mansion every twenty-four hours.

First Mansion

0 Aries–12 Aries 51

This is the spring equinox, when the days and nights are of equal length. It is likely to be a day of arguments but also of travel, either physical or spiritual journeys.

Second Mansion

12 Aries 51–25 Aries 42

People can find treasure and valued items that they have lost.

Third Mansion

25 Aries 42–8 Taurus 34

This is a good time for hunting or sailing. If a shaman needs to make up some herbal medicine or use some form of alchemy, this is a good day for it.

Fourth Mansion

8 Taurus 34–21 Taurus 25

Buildings, fountains, springs, wells, and even mines might be shaken or destroyed on this day. Insects and small animals may leave the area, and everyone is likely to be in a bad mood.

Fifth Mansion

21 Taurus 25–4 Gemini 17

This is a good time to build something. Those who have been ill will recover, and there will be a good-natured and pleasant atmosphere all around.

Sixth Mansion

4 Gemini 17–17 Gemini 8

Hunting will be successful, but other endeavors may not be. The weather may damage crops or fruit. Shamanic healers won't get anywhere and are advised to leave their work for a better time.

Seventh Mansion

17 Gemini 8–0 Cancer

This is the beginning of summer solstice, when days are at their longest. This time is good for friends and lovers and for success in trade, but it is not a great time for legal matters. It is said that flies can be driven away at this time.

Eighth Mansion

0 Cancer–12 Cancer 51

This is the passing of the summer solstice. It is a good time for lovers, friendship, and welcoming travelers. It is also a good time in which to put lawbreakers in prison and for ridding an area of mice.

Ninth Mansion

12 Cancer 51–25 Cancer 42

This is a bad time all around—everyone will be in a touchy and irritable mood. Travel won't go well, and there may be trouble with crops.

Tenth Mansion

25 Cancer 42–8 Leo 34

This is a good time to rebuild or strengthen existing buildings. It is also good for love, generosity, and asking others for help, especially when it comes to having people on your side if there is a battle to be fought.

Eleventh Mansion

8 Leo 34–21 Leo 25

This is a great time for any form of trade, so it is good for buying and selling goods, or taking trips for business.

Twelfth Mansion

21 Leo 25–4 Virgo 17

This is a good time for land-based matters, such as crops and animals, but not for sailors or fishing. If you employ others to do work, whether as staff or friends who lend a hand, they will be very helpful.

Thirteenth Mansion

4 Virgo 17–17 Virgo 8

This is an all-around great time for good luck, abundance, travel, and harvests.

Fourteenth Mansion

17 Virgo 8–0 Libra

This is the autumnal equinox, when the days and nights are once again of equal length. It is an excellent time for most things, especially for marriage and family life, for curing the sick, and for trips over water—but it is not so good for travel over land.

Fifteenth Mansion

0 Libra–12 Libra 51

Mining and digging should go well now, as should such activities as pulling down worn-out structures that need to be replaced. It is a good time to settle disputes and even to divorce, but it isn't so good for those who have to travel.

Sixteenth Mansion

12 Libra 51–25 Libra 42

This is a bad time for travel and definitely a bad time for weddings. Crops and animals may develop problems today, and it will be hard to sell any.

Seventeenth Mansion

25 Libra 42–8 Scorpio 34

If the community has suffered a period of bad luck, things will improve now. Matters concerning love, marriage, and relationships in general will go well, and construction work will succeed. Anyone who needs to cross water for any reason will be successful.

Eighteenth Mansion

8 Scorpio 34–21 Scorpio 25

The elders of the community will fall out with each other and with other neighbors. There may even be a conspiracy to get rid of someone who is in charge. However, it is a beneficial time for those who don't have any seniority.

Nineteenth Mansion

21 Scorpio 25–4 Sagittarius 17

If the tribe has to confront others now, it will win.

Twentieth Mansion

4 Sagittarius 17–17 Sagittarius 8

This is a good time in which to break in wild horses, but it could be bad for the community's finances.

Twenty-First Mansion

17 Sagittarius 8–0 Capricorn

This is the winter solstice, when the days are at their shortest. It is good for preserving foodstuffs for the winter, for repairing buildings, and for travel, but there will be discord among married people and even divorces to follow.

Twenty-Second Mansion

0 Capricorn–12 Capricorn 51

This is a good time for shamanic healing and curing diseases.

Twenty-Third Mansion

12 Capricorn 51–25 Capricorn 42

Those who are sick will start to feel much better, but it is not a good time for relationships, and some couples may decide to part.

Twenty-Fourth Mansion

25 Capricorn 42–8 Aquarius 34

This is a good time for couples and for marriage. However, it will be hard for the elders to do their job and it may be difficult to dispense justice.

Twenty-Fifth Mansion

8 Aquarius 34–21 Aquarius 25

There is an angry feel to this phase, and it puts everyone in a bad temper. Some people will want vengeance against others, and some relationships will break up. However, important messages will get through, and everyone in the community will remember to do their duty. It is a bad time for spellcasting.

Twenty-Sixth Mansion

21 Aquarius 25–4 Pisces 17

This is a bad time for anyone working on carpentry or home repairs, or trying to work in harmony with others.

Twenty-Seventh Mansion

4 Pisces 17–17 Pisces 8

Anything to do with food production or bringing money and goods into the community will go well, but other areas of work won't be so successful, such as building or traveling on water.

Twenty-Eighth Mansion

17 Pisces 8–0 Aries

We have returned to the spring equinox. It is a good time to plan the crops and hunt for the coming year and a good time for all-around happiness. Travelers are protected, but anything that the community sets out to buy will turn out to be more expensive than expected.

❋ ❋ ❋

CONCLUSION

I hope by the time you have reached the end of this book that it has awakened something within you and that you will continue on this path, enjoy learning more about yourself, and keep expanding your consciousness. Now that you understand some of the ways and practices in shamanism, you can create a more peaceful and simple way of life for yourself, integrating some of it into your routine by spending more time in nature and tuning in to the spirits of trees, plants, and animals.

When you are ready to learn more, the teacher often appears—whether in physical or in spiritual form—to help you with your journeys to other realms. This will help you to find your spirit animal, connect you to your ancestors and spirit guides, and be more open to new opportunities and events. Just spend a little more quiet time in nature or time alone to focus inward in order to discover the things that are right for you and that resonate with you.

I wish you all the luck in your onward journey. May it truly enrich your life.

ABOUT THE AUTHOR

Tracie Long began to see and hear spirits when she was about six years old, and she went through her teens and twenties feeling very different from most people. It wasn't until she was in her early thirties that she finally embraced her gift. Like many psychics and mediums, she has spent a long time practicing and studying, and she has now been working in the mind, body, spirit industry for almost thirty years.

Tracie specializes in tarot, angels, spiritual development, meditation, shamanic healing and coaching, and moon cycles. She has worked with sensitive children, and run a few paranormal investigations, but today she is most often called upon to help spirits who are stuck or causing problems for families to pass over. She also tutors alongside the Spiritual Workers Association, was a chairwoman of the British Astrological and Psychic Society from 2017–2018, has a BTEC in business management, and, in 2011, completed a teaching degree.

INDEX

IMAGE CREDITS